"One hundred of my wives got out of debt because of this book!"

— King Solomon

"I should have read this book! It's hot where I am!"

—The Rich Young Rulers

what you **didn't** learn
from your parents about

money

[a guide to a pricey subject]

matthew paul turner

TH1NK
P.O. Box 35001
Colorado Springs, Colorado 80935

TH1NK is an imprint of NavPress.
TH1NK and the TH1NK logo are registered trademarks of NavPress. Absence of ®
in connection with marks of NavPress or other parties does not indicate an absence of
registration of those marks.

ISBN-10: 1-57683-941-9
ISBN-13: 9-78157683-941-6

Cover design by Brand Navigation, LLC: DeAnna Pierce, Terra Petersen,
    and Bill Chiaravalle, www.brandnavigation.com
Cover image by CSA Images
Creative Team: Nicci Hubert, Kathy Mosier, Arvid Wallen, Laura Spray, Pat Reinheimer

Turner, Matthew Paul, 1973-
   What you didn't learn from your parents about money : a guide to
a pricey subject / Matthew Paul Turner.
      p. cm.
   Includes bibliographical references.
   ISBN 1-57683-941-9
   1. Finance, Personal--Religious aspects--Christianity. 2. Invest-
ments--Religious aspects--Christianity.   I. Title.
HG179.T87 2007
332.024--dc22

FOR A FREE CATALOG OF NAVPRESS BOOKS & BIBLE STUDIES,
    CALL 1-800-366-7788 (USA) OR 1-800-839-4769 (CANADA)

Contents

Disclaimer

**This book will not make you rich.
Well, it won't unless you buy a whole bunch
and begin selling them out of the trunk of your car.**

Acknowledgments

I would like to thank:

- $ Jessica, my bride, for putting up with my handling of money
- $ All of my family and friends
- $ Everyone who shared their thoughts and stories with me for this book
- $ Nicci and Kathy at TH1NK Books for pushing me on this one
- $ Everyone at NavPress for making me feel loved [Special thanks to Kate B., Brent, Erin, Toby, and Kate E. for a great CBA meal]
- $ Calculators for adding, subtracting, multiplying, and dividing, and for always being right

Pop Culture and Money Trivia!
[a quick game of trivia to get us started]

Question #1: Can you name the theme song for Donald Trump's *The Apprentice* and the band that originally performed it?

Question #2: Damon Wayans wrote and directed what 1992 comedy about the lust for cash?

Question #3: What 1997 film has grossed nearly $601 million in the U.S., more than any other film?

Question #4: How much money does each player get at the beginning of a game of Monopoly?

Introduction
[in money terms, this is your first paycheck]

Money never made a man happy yet,
nor will it.
There is nothing in its nature
to produce happiness.
The more a man has, the more he wants.
Instead of it filling a vacuum, it makes one.
— Benjamin Franklin

Just in case you failed to notice the picture of a money tree on the cover [*go ahead, look at the cover again*], it might be good for you to know that you're indeed holding a book *about* money. And, yes, that's why this book is green. Of course, I realize that the color *green* as it relates to money in the United States might not make as much sense as it would have several years ago when money was all green. But certainly you *remember* when U.S. currency was *completely green*, right? If not, ask your grandpa about the "good ole days." He'll tell you how great it was when money was all green.

Today our bills look more like a bowl of Fruity Pebbles, a rainbow of pretty pastels.

Anyway, before you become frustrated and deflated because you're reading a book about money, I should tell you that this isn't your ordinary book about money. Well, okay, so it is kind of an ordinary book about money, but I believe you'll have a lot more fun reading this book than any book by Suze Orman [she's that financial guru with the crazy haircut—you know, the one where you're not sure whether she's trying to say, "I love Ellen!" or "Let us never forget Dorothy Hamill!"].

But if you've chosen to purchase this book [or steal it, borrow it, or borrow it and keep it, which is pretty much stealing], then you're at least somewhat interested in the subject of money. Okay, so I could be lying to myself about this, but let's all pretend we're interested in the subject of money.

YES?!?

[ding, ding, ding]

 LET'S GET STARTED.

More than likely by the time you were six years old, you knew a little about money. Of course, you didn't know much, but it certainly was enough to know that having it was a lot more fun than *not* having it.

Am I right?

Of course, when you were six, having it usually meant that you waited around for ten-dollar bills from Grandma on your birthday or prayed that your baby teeth began to come loose so the tooth fairy would visit. However, some of us weren't patient enough to wait, so instead we went searching for spare change around the house like it was buried treasure.

When you're a kid, the size of coins matter. You're not aware that the dime is actually worth more than the nickel, but you definitely know that the quarter is the mother of all coins.

And as a kid, I learned early that being "rich" had its share of rules. When I was seven, my friend Alicia came over to my house. While our parents chatted, she and I counted all my loose change and rolled it. It was fun because we used one of those cool devices that separates pennies, nickels, dimes, and quarters into slots. We were fascinated as we watched my coins skim down the plastic slide into their respective places. To us, that coin-separating device was better than Atari.

But right in the middle of counting my loot, my father walked into the room. When I saw him, I smiled big and said, "Hey, Dad, LOOK! I've already counted $21.50! And there's still more to count. I'm giving Alicia a couple rolls because I have so much!"

Dad looked at me a little less enthusiastically than I imagined he would.

"Matthew, it's not polite to talk about how much money you have," said Dad. "You shouldn't brag." Dad didn't say it in a mean tone, but sometimes his nice tone was still a little scary. Not *Texas Chainsaw Massacre* scary; more like John Wayne.

Dad was smart when it came to money, and he taught me a lot. When I was eight, in an effort to teach me the value of money *and* to help me save for college, my father bought me twelve chickens and a coop. Until I was thirteen, I was in the business of selling eggs to all the old ladies in my church. This made me not only rather wealthy for my age but also *super* cool. Being the youngest chicken farmer in my county had a lot of privileges. [☺ sarcasm implied] But my "cool" occupation wasn't all bad.

By the time I was fourteen, after five years of selling eggs and with the help of a couple of good certificates of deposit,* I had saved more than $6,000 for college. My dad's lesson

---

* *According to Investopedia.com, a certificate of deposit is defined as "a savings certificate entitling the bearer to receive interest. A CD bears a maturity date, a specified fixed interest rate and can be issued in any denomination. CDs are generally issued by commercial banks and are insured by the FDIC. The term of a CD generally ranges from one month to five years."*

did allow me to save money for college, but, sadly, purchasing and maintaining a chicken coop for all those years probably cost him just as much. And, truthfully, I didn't learn all that much about money's *value*, though I did learn about hard work. [And, as a bonus, I know a lot of random facts about chickens—more than any guy with noncallused hands should be privy to.]

Of course, Dad could have given me $6,000 and avoided the reality of a chicken coop, which included shooting rats, spraying for chicken lice, cutting the heads off large black snakes, and shoveling tons of chicken poop. But Dad saw value in teaching me what it means to earn money; he wanted me to learn that money *doesn't grow on trees*.

And Dad didn't mind the extra responsibility; he *loved* to work more than any individual I knew. On weekends, Dad's motto was "It's Saturday; thou shalt get up early and work your butt off." Dad's whole "work being fun" thing was extremely difficult for me to understand when I was young. To him, hard work was like the eleventh commandment. To this day, he gets excited about work like other people get excited about vacations. Dad would much rather clean the crap out of a chicken coop than go to the mall, to an amusement park, or camping.

Not all of Dad's money lessons required physical labor. Some of his money wisdom came in bite-sized sayings. For instance, whenever he and I talked about dating, he'd always chime in with his financial wisdom.

"Is the girl you're interested in rich, son?" he'd ask me with a tone that made it difficult to know whether or not he was being serious.

"It's as easy to love a rich woman as it is a poor one, buck! Make sure you remember that!"

I do think Dad was kidding when he basically told me to marry a rich woman, but at times I wasn't sure. My father sometimes mixed his truth and humor like a politician. However, Dad indeed taught me a lot about money—the normal stuff like saving, tithing, investing, giving, and budgeting. I actually did listen sometimes, but putting Dad's advice into practice often proved to be a difficult task. And between you and me, my mom's way of thinking about money compared to Dad's mind-set is, umm, how can I say this respectfully? A lot more *free*, so to speak.

Now, Mom was certainly not foolish with money; she just had a lot more fun with it. While Dad was extremely conservative, frugal, and practical, Mom was less rigid, prone to have a frivolous financial moment once in a while, and much more willing to give money away. These differences between my parents certainly made life in the Turner home a little interesting. Some of Mom and Dad's more *passionate* conversations revolved around spending, saving, and whether or not Mom truly needed that new "fashion statement."

Those family dynamics perhaps taught me more about money than the actual advice and lectures I heard from my parents. Whether we like it or not, our parents leave their financial thumbprint on our lives. Obviously this can be a positive *or* negative reality. In most cases, however, it's both. Whether you're eighteen or thirty-five, your parents—each of them individually as well as together—have played a pretty integral role in how you view money. [See the questions on pages 27–29 to consider how your parents may have affected you!]

For some of you, talking about money is like getting your wisdom teeth pulled out by a guy who smells like burnt hair. Have you ever had that happen to you? *Trust me, it's awful!*

And I'll be honest: This little financial chat we're about to engage in for the next two hundred pages or so might make you—and me—feel a wee bit uncomfortable. [Whispering: *It feels kind of like we're both sitting around in our underwear. And neither of us wants to be in our underwear. Well, at least I don't. YOU might!*] Unfortunately, talking about money can get personal and make one feel a little vulnerable [⏚ I know this from experience]. Of course, I'm not going to embarrass you. I said it would be uncomfortable, *not* cruel. It won't be uncomfortable like having to drop your pants in front of your doctor is uncomfortable. However, because this book is about money, you might feel a bit squeamish when thinking and [hopefully] rethinking your current financial lifestyle.

If this is you, I understand your situation. It was only a year or two ago that I began to discuss the truth about my financial situation—the good *and* the bad. Sometimes just hearing a financial "pro" talk about the dangers of debt overwhelms me with anxiety. Honestly, there have been a couple times while listening to Dave Ramsey's [☺ one of those financial pros] radio show that I've looked for a nearby high bridge to jump from. Ha ha ha. I'm just kidding. *Gosh, you take me SO seriously!* Lighten up!

Here's the deal: Fear can tempt us to shut down and resist thinking about and responding to the issues our financial situation entails. But beyond the fear—if we're willing to push through it—is the financial lifestyle that God has designed.

And you know what that means; it means that you, as a follower of Jesus, need to pursue that lifestyle. But here comes the hard part: Pursuing will require you to work through the fear of talking about money. Because if you never face the fear, you'll never find the healthy financial balance you're looking for.

Now, some of you are just the opposite of what I've been talking about; you'll actually enjoy this conversation about money. In fact, discussing finances is something you look forward to, something that drives your inner need for success. Whenever a money conversation happens, you're front and center, sharing with all your friends your wisdom about personal investments and your best advice about savings, and bragging about all of your accomplishments. [☺☞ Psst! Hey, you! I hate to break it to you, but all of your friends are calling you *obnoxious* behind your back. Just thought I'd share. Hey, man, we're cool like that.]

Though you might be the type of person who's unafraid of a little chat about money, try to resist thinking about this little book as simply a review of what you already know. Sure, you might be aware of the "basics," things like investing, banking, and how to buy a house. And though I'll certainly be talking about the basics to money, I'll also be discussing the spiritual aspects of money. As I'm sure you know [because you're *very* smart], our thinking about money isn't simply

What's in Your Wallet?

Capital One might be praying your wallet contains its Visa card, but according to a study by the University of California at San Francisco, there's a decent chance your wallet contains a lot more than just credit cards, pictures of your loved ones, and a driver's license. If you carry money — coins *or* notes — in your wallet, you might also be carrying fecal bacteria, E. coli, and Staphylococcus aureus. [☙ Lucky us, some of us are carrying this bacterial gem in our noses! *Yuck!*] In Japan, money is known to be so dirty that special cleaning ATMs have been developed where you can get your money "laundered" using heat or disinfectant chemicals.[1]

about knowing financial facts or having business savvy; it's also about understanding our call as people of faith to invest in the culture. Sometimes those of us who "know" money focus too much on making another buck or *thinking we know everything there is to know about steward-ship* rather than on how we can continue on the journey toward knowing how to better serve God with our finances. In other words, we should be using that good money sense for the good of God's kingdom.

I'd be lying if I didn't admit to sometimes misunderstanding and struggling with God's perspective on money. [Am I a good confessor, or what? I mean, who else in the Christian author world confesses to his ineptness quicker than I do? Huh? *Who?* No, really, answer that question. *No, not Philip Yancey!*] Money is a complicated topic, one for which people have a lot of different views and opin-ions. But like it does for many complicated subjects — umm, ones like peacemaking, the vagina, and fleas — Scripture does give us some direction on money. Okay, so the Bible doesn't really talk much about fleas. *And my editor says it doesn't mention the vagina too often either.* But if you're looking for info on peacemaking, you're totally covered! The Bible's information on money is not necessarily a well-defined road map; it doesn't mention stocks, bonds, and 401ks. But God's Word does offer principles for how we should think about money, and his plan isn't a get-rich, blessing-dosed, we-all-get-to-be-philanthropists kind of plan. *Whew! Or most of us would be out of his plan right now, huh?*

And I'd be lying if I didn't admit that this book is as much for me as it is for you. [You see? *Such a good confessor!* Heck, you think I confess well in *this* book? You should check out what I confess in *What You Didn't Learn from Your Parents About Sex.*]

Okay, this might be a little shocking, but I wasn't necessarily sold on writing a book about money. In fact, I disliked the idea — *a lot.* You might be wondering why, then, I decided to write this book. The short answer is this: I felt this book was needed.

And this surprised me, really. I mean, I'm the first to admit that seldom is a book *truly* needed. And when it comes to the topic of money, the need for another book seems even less likely. Books on money are a dime a dozen. Just visit a bookstore;

literally thousands of titles about every possible money subject exist in today's book market. Almost everybody—at least most people who know *anything* about finances—has written a book sharing his or her expertise on money.

So what the heck am I doing writing a book about money? [*The Lord only knows!*] I mean, I'm not an expert, and I probably never will be. I'm not rich, and, honestly, considering that I'm a writer in the Christian publishing world, I don't see that happening. I've made at least a thousand financial mistakes in my life so far, some of which I've corrected, others that I'm still working out. But perhaps the biggest issue is the fact that sometimes I still cringe at the thought of talking about money, not to mention the thought of researching and writing an entire book on the topic.

However, I kind of dislike the way many other books talk about money. Books in the mainstream publishing world make money seem like it's a god, something all of us should crave, sacrifice for, and do whatever it takes to get. Most of these kinds of financial books, due to the fact that financial experts [or famous rich people] wrote them, tend to read like you're sitting in one of those annoying motivational conventions, the ones where the speaker wears a blue power suit, has a "Britney" microphone hooked to his ear, and talks as if everyone should be living and pursuing the wealthy life just like he is. Too often these books focus on getting wealthy, staying wealthy, and then getting wealthier. [Whispering: *Your Best Life Now*! But you didn't hear me say that out loud in this book!]

I'll be the first to admit that, based on the few occasions when my personal bank account was somewhat healthy, having money feels pretty good. But ole Ben Franklin*—despite his quote basically ripping off Proverbs without attribution—was on to something: Money *doesn't* bring happiness. Or at least that's what most of us have heard our entire lives. But let's be frank: Money certainly can disguise itself as such—maybe not *true* happiness, but definitely something that feels very close, something that too many of us think is sufficient.

As you probably know, those of us who follow Jesus are called to think about money with the kingdom in mind. Money shouldn't be a means toward comfort, success, power, and prosperity. If you're looking to read a book that's about becoming rich and living a prosperous life, this isn't it. As much as we hear about "financial blessing" from many well-respected

---

* *Quick thought: I wonder if Mr. Franklin would still believe money fails to bring happiness if he were to experience the thrill of what can be bought inside an Apple store. I mean, come on, everything Mac is more addictive than porn. Now, I'm not suggesting the lure of an iPod would cause him to wobble on his claim, but I believe it would be much more difficult for him to put his own words into practice had he lived in the twenty-first century. My guess is that he would have had an iPod—or would have at least been tempted to invent it. It's just a thought.*

church leaders, I personally cannot find in Scripture where Jesus teaches that his followers are promised financial prosperity here on earth. And it certainly *isn't* part of the gospel. But don't misunderstand me. I'm not against financial gain; this isn't a book about all of us pursuing the life of a homeless person. However, I do hope that while we study money together, each of us will discover how God would have us as individuals *think* about money.

No, I'm not an expert, but I've witnessed firsthand what money can do—both the good and the bad.

Money is a frustrating topic. All of the questions, thoughts, and fears we experience when talking about money are quite normal. Money is one of those subjects that seems to get more and more complicated as we get older. The thing with money is this: When you have a lot, it's a difficult journey. But when you have a little, it's an equally difficult journey. Interestingly enough, *having* money doesn't tend to be the problem we face. Well, it isn't unless you're an heir to a million-dollar company or you've developed some mega-popular Internet site or you're just filthy rich by default, like Prince Harry. For the rest of us, the problems we experience are about keeping, saving, giving, investing, losing, making, and *not* having money. On top of that, many of us become jealous, catty, prideful, nosey, controlling, lustful, and selfish—all because of money.

Whether you're in college, you just graduated, or you're learning to exist in the career world, each of your life experiences offers new challenges, new chances for mistakes, and more "advice" than you can mentally consume. However, each experience also provides the opportunity to begin again, a new chance to pursue wisdom and work toward becoming financially healthy as you learn to serve God and his kingdom with your money.

Here's to all of us learning the practical and spiritual aspects of money—in other words, the important stuff our parents didn't teach us about money [or did, but we failed to listen].

Matthew
matthew@dottedline.net
www.matthewpaulturner.com
www.myspace.com/MPTBooks

PS: I promise to try to make this conversation as enjoyable as possible, but, hey, it's about money, and I'm not a miracle worker. But I will try.

Before we move on to section 1, I think it would be good for you to think for a couple of minutes about how your parents influenced the way you think about and handle money.

Just in case you think the twenty-dollar bill your grandmother sent you for your birthday is a fake [🕊 the chances of this being true is, according to the Federal Reserve Bank of Atlanta, Georgia, 3/100ths of 1 percent[2]], here are a few tips from the U.S. Secret Service that might help you figure out whether your gift from Granny is counterfeit. You up for this little exercise? Take out Granny's twenty and see if you can recognize the following features:

☒ If it's the real thing, the portrait [🖼 since it's a twenty, it should be Andrew Jackson] and the picture on the back of the note should stand out noticeably from the background [a little like those 3D images that were *really* popular in the midnineties, but not exactly], and Andrew's eyes in the picture should appear lifelike! [👻 spoooooooky] If the bill is a fake, the pictures may merge with the background, the eyes or other parts of Andrew's face may be dull or smudged, and he might appear unusually white.

☒ They also suggest you notice the print job. According to those who know money, on *true* currency, "Numbers are firmly, evenly printed and well spaced, and the fine crisscrossing lines of the scrollwork borders are sharp and unbroken." [😵 Did you get all that? It kind of confused me.]

☒ According to our government, our currency is printed on high-quality paper made of 75 percent cotton and 25 percent linen [to help sustain its durability], and if it's the real thing, you should be able to see tiny red and blue [USA! USA!] fibers embedded in the paper. However, they do warn that these may not be visible if the bill is badly worn or dirty [see sidebar on page 20 for what that dirt might be]. On a counterfeit bill, the red and blue lines might be drawn or printed.

☒ Lastly, they suggest that rubbing the bill against white paper to see if it smudges is *not* an effective way to tell if it's a fake. Apparently, real money will sometimes leave a mark![3]

If you think your grandmother did indeed pass you a fake twenty, make sure you tell her you're *very* disappointed in her behavior [😠 but be kind; yes, she's a felon, but she's also your granny]. After that, haul her butt into the closest police station and tell the chief that Granny's been bad.

Perhaps you've never seriously considered how your parents might have affected your outlook on money. But you need to think about it! Because it's important! Like seriously, if you suck at handling money, there's a good chance you could totally be blaming your parents for a certain percentage of your total suckage. Now, I'm not recommending you do that, but I just said you *could* be blaming your parents. And I'm not going to make you get all deep and contemplative about this, but I do think it would be helpful, before we begin talking about the basics of money, for you to consider the following questions. And, more important than the questions, the *answers* to the following questions. [Please journal your answers or use the spaces provided.]

Key Questions to Consider Regarding Parents and Money!

1. On a scale from one to ten [ten being the best], how do you perceive your parents' handling of money?

2. How did you perceive your overall financial situation as a child? In other words, did you think of your family as wealthy, moderately wealthy, middle-class, lower-middle-class, or poor?

3. Did that perceived status [the answer to question 2] have any effect on your self-esteem? For example, were you teased for being poor? Were you ever embarrassed by your family's wealth?

4. When it came to the topic of money, how did your parents interact with each other? Did they talk about it openly? Was it a private issue? Did they argue about finances a lot? Was money always a stressful topic?

5. Was debt ever a problem for your parents? If so, how did their debt affect you [if at all]?

6. Did your parents ever buy you stuff despite being unable to afford it? Did this make you feel guilty? Did you ever *ask* them to buy you something they couldn't afford?

7. Did your parents experience any good or bad *major* financial events? Bankruptcy? Stock-market crash? Lottery win? Overnight success? Loss of a job? If so, how did the experience[s] affect you?

8. When it came to money, were your parents frugal, tight, wasteful?

9. How generous were your parents? Did they tithe or support charities or any other worthy causes?

10. Did your parents offer any *specific* advice to you about money? If so, what was that advice?

11. When you think about your current financial habits, how do you see your parents' decisions—good or bad—affecting you?

Okay, so how you answered those questions certainly can start to give you an idea of how your parents' financial lifestyle might have influenced your current financial habits. Sometimes our parents' guidance lends itself nicely toward creating a healthy money mind-set; other times our parents' thinking about money is about as healthy as licking a doorknob. [Of course, I rarely see anyone licking a doorknob, but I hear it happens once in a while, and I hear it's very unhealthy.] Most of our parents probably land somewhere in the middle. Sure, we can see where our parents have made mistakes, but we can also see how their influence has helped us on our journey

What Did You Learn From Mom and Dad?

[twentysomethings offer their thoughts]

⇨ "Mom and Dad were pretty cool when it came to money. Mom made me start a savings account when I was thirteen. Forty percent of what I made went into my savings, 10 percent went to the church, and I was allowed to use the rest on things I needed."
— Jeff, 22, graduate student in South Dakota

⇨ "I learned how to shop! My mother spent more money on clothes than any woman I know, and, unfortunately, I kind of got that gene."
— Katie, 26, personal assistant for a lawmaker in Florida

⇨ "My family was pretty well off. So I always had everything I wanted when I was a kid. I think that definitely caused me to be pretty spoiled for a long time and really gave me little concept as to how to manage my money. My first few years out of college were rough."
— Aaron, 28, manager at the Gap

toward financial wellness. Take a second to think about these three BIG areas in our lives that parents often influence.

1 Spending. Whether your parents were spendthrifts [which is a weird combo of words to describe someone who spends money unwisely, but look it up, it's the right word], cheap, or simply ultraconservative, how we watched our parents utilize their funds will directly affect our spending habits. Now, this could work one of two ways: (1) You might have followed in your parents' footsteps and done exactly what they did in the past, *or* (2) You might go in the opposite direction of your parents [either out of spite or out of stupidity!].

2 Financial ego. If your parents flaunted their wealth like Joan Rivers flaunts bad plastic surgery, you might be tempted to do the same [😑 very ugly]. As you probably know, how we "wear" our money is quite often a *learned* behavior, and it can be either tasteful or gaudy or downright obnoxious. When we start making *real* money, our egos tend to be affected by our protruding bank accounts. How we witnessed our parents portraying wealth is often how we will expose to the world our cash flow.

Pointless Fact

In the NIV version of the Bible, the word *money* is mentioned 112 times! In the NLT? 197 times! KJV? 123 times! *The Message*? 162 times!

>>**Okay, I have a story:** Several years ago a buddy of mine won $50,000 in a scratch-off lottery game. My friend hadn't seen this kind of cash before; he was a "good-ole boy" from my hometown. He certainly wasn't born poverty stricken, but he was no heir to Rockefeller either. So when he won $50K — which isn't a huge lottery win — he did what a lot of people would do: He splurged. He bought a truck, a boat, and a gun [a shotgun to be exact], and he put $2K down on a credit card. While I was visiting my parents about five months after his big win, he and I got together.

It didn't take long for me to notice a few changes in Ted's personality.

When pulling into my parents' driveway, he let the entire community know he had arrived by revving the engine to his brand-new, fully loaded Ford F-150. Upon entering the house, Ted made sure we knew his new ride had a remote-control starter key. As Ted walked through our kitchen door, he shrugged his shoulders and said, "Darn, I keep forgetting to turn off my new truck."

He then proceeded to pull a small contraption out of his pocket and push a red button. "That should do it."

Suddenly the friend I had known since I was six was showing off the things he had bought with his new money. Only a few months earlier, Ted was a pretty humble guy with an average income. Now, a few new "toys" had given my friend an ego, and it was ugly. And you know what? Despite his money being long gone, his ego is still in place. How convenient! **Okay, back to your regularly scheduled content.** <<

3 **Generosity.** If your parents were open-handed with their finances, this usually means you'll gravitate toward being generous also. This isn't always the rule, but when a generous spirit is a natural part of our lives, it is often a learned behavior. On the other hand, if your parents were selfish, this, too, is a learned behavior [😣 sucks to be you *and* everyone else around you].

Now, these three subjects are hardly the extent of how your parents might have affected you; the influence of moms and dads is quite flexible and can reach into almost every aspect of our financial lifestyle, whether we know it or not. Only you know to what degree your parents have influenced you and whether that influence is good or bad. If your parents passed down mostly *positive* money tactics, you should thank God because you are indeed blessed. However, as a result of your parents' negative influence, how you pursue a godly mind-set and healthy habits can become a little more complicated. Of course, you might be apt to feel the necessity to panic! But don't, at least not yet. Continue reading. If you still feel the need to panic after reading this book, please feel free to do it at your leisure! Of course, you might also consider counseling *or marrying rich.*

[That was a joke. Not a *good* joke but a joke nonetheless.]

Now on to section 1! All right! Totally! *Hotness!*

Rethinking Money

[a few things about God, money, and God and money]

When it is a question
of money, everybody is
of the same religion.

— Voltaire

Almighty Dollar/Almighty God: You Can't Worship Both

We work hard for our money.* [🎧 Yes, this is a cliché. You know what a cliché is, right? It's when something is totally overused? I've always wanted to invent a cliché. I think that would be hot.]

But it's not always a true cliché. Some people get handed financial gain on a silver platter — a platter from Tiffany's, no doubt. Some win the lottery, *like my friend Ted*. Some do a lot of inappropriate things to make money, *like sell their bodies*. Yeah, I don't have to tell you; you know you're a *sinner*! But most of us work our butts off to make a buck, hoping our hard work will pay off in the form of a nice home with a two-car garage, a few luxury items, a couple of vacations to Cancun, and a sweet retirement. Yeah, *AND AN IPOD!!! Can't forget the iPod!*

That's part of the American dream, right? Well, at least that's the message we've been told.

But how do we get this so-called *dream life*? [🖐 insert a hint of sarcasm here] Well, most of us work forty — some

---

* If the "we" in this first sentence is replaced with "she" and the word "our" with "the," you've almost *got the title of a 1983 hit song by Donna Summer — "She Works Hard for the Money"! Ha ha!*

of us fifty, sixty, seventy—hours a week for corporations, the government, retail stores, service-oriented companies, ministries, and the list goes on. If we're lucky, our jobs come with a decent salary, benefits, a good 401k plan, two weeks of paid vacation, and hopefully some fulfillment, enjoyment, and community. Again, *that's* if you're lucky [or *blessed*, as we Christians like to say].

>>**Okay, can I say something here?** I just want to clear something up right here and now. Get ready; this might come as a shock to a couple of you. But I think it's really important. Okay, here it goes: The American dream, you know the one I just made reference to? Yeah, it's not biblical. Did you get that one? Umm, don't hit me for saying that. I only said it because I love you. [Or at least I am pretending to love you for the sake of this book!] I just don't want you to be led astray. It can get crazy pursuing that dream. I know it's hard to believe, especially considering that a lot of American evangelicals think this country is like a new Israel, a new "Promised Land," or pre-heaven. Now, I'm not suggesting that this dream is sinful and evil to pursue; it's simply not a biblical promise. We still friends? I hope so. **Okay, back to the book.**<<

Though the dream of financial success is not sinful, humans can get lost when pursuing it. We see this happen all the time. Even those of us who follow Jesus can become overwhelmed with a lust for success, power, and luxury; sometimes it becomes so great that we're willing to invest *whatever it takes* to make the dream a reality. Some of us capture the dream full-on, and our investments pay off. Some of us fail—not miserably, but we just don't end up getting where we want to be. But the desire, the lust for all the things money can bring, still burns inside of us. No matter whether we're living the dream, wanting more of it, still chasing it, or bitter because of it, we can become lost.

Here's one of the first basics of money as it relates to being Christian:

"You can't worship two gods at once. Loving one god, you'll end up hating the other. Adoration of one feeds contempt for the other. You can't worship God and Money both."

Just in case you're wondering, Jesus said those words, not me (Matthew 6:24, MSG). *Go Jesus! You're feeling convicted, aren't you?* But I know how much they hurt. So that you're not confused, it might be helpful for me to mention that you are completely able to worship money or to worship God. It's just impossible to do both simultaneously. Sadly, so many of us try, but we always fail.

Are you ready for a question? [not this one]

WHAT WOULD YOU BE WILLING TO DO FOR MONEY?

I know that sounds a little like the "What would you do for a Klondike bar?" commercial. Do you remember that commercial? It was one of my favorites as a kid. That one guy with the bad hairpiece . . . Okay, *my editor* tells me you're not interested in my silly story. She's making me get back to the content. [Whispering: *You should e-mail me and I'll give you her e-mail address and then you can send her a mean little letter!*] But truly, think about that question for a little bit. As you're thinking, I'm going to keep writing, but I promise to come back to this inquiry in a few moments. [You're thinking, right? Okay, good.]

On a recent trip from Nashville down to Birmingham, Alabama, my wife and I witnessed a middle-aged man running across a very busy I-65. "What in the world is this idiot doing?" my wife, who was driving [at eighty miles per hour], screamed. As an entire line of fast-moving traffic screeched to a stop, the "idiot" ran safely to the other side. However, though he had made it safely to the other side, it seemed the man wasn't finished with his little fear factor routine [☺ for him and us]. We could tell he was looking for a chance to make another pass. But as we drove by—*slowly*—the idiot's quest began to make sense [well, sort of]. The *reason* he was running across four lanes of busy highway [and getting ready to do it again] suddenly flew underneath our car and landed in the middle of the road behind us. The man was trying to chase down some cash. Hopefully it was

 at least fifty dollars, since he was risking his life. But I wasn't so sure; it looked like a one-dollar bill to me.

Was that man worshiping his money out there on the highway? Maybe not. But it raises an interesting thought: Does a willingness to do almost anything for money imply a worship of it? Face it: People will do just about anything* for a few extra bucks. I've witnessed this to be true on so many occasions. Most of us have probably watched our friends prepping to do something incredibly stupid for money. In fact, some of us have even warned them *not* to do it. But they did it anyway. And because they walked away with one hundred dollars in their pockets, hindsight made their acts seem not quite as stupid. Of course, as the dollar amount increases, the more stupid [or daring or pathetic] many of us are willing to become. I've seen people do all kinds of things for money—strip, test their fear of heights, strip and then run around campus, swallow strange bugs, drink enough beer that vomiting is induced, skydive and strip and then dance on a table. For some reason when I was in college, I had quite a few friends willing to take their clothes off for money [and it was never *that* much money].

---

* I once swallowed a goldfish for twenty bucks. [And then I never got paid.]

However, a little nudity [the kind that's not related to sexual promiscuity] is simply the tip of the iceberg when it comes to what we're willing to do to possess more money. Perhaps this would be a good time to bring up that question again.

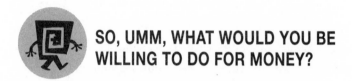

SO, UMM, WHAT WOULD YOU BE WILLING TO DO FOR MONEY?

I know it's a little difficult to answer. Would it make it easier if I were holding one thousand dollars in front of your face? Before you do answer, consider these questions: Would you move to another state for more money? How about to Asia? Would you leave your family and friends for more money? Would you do something illegal? Would you sacrifice time with your husband or wife, girlfriend or boyfriend, or best friend in hopes of making more money? Would you perform a sexual favor for money? Would your *willingness* change as the amount of money being offered increased?

Remember the movie *Indecent Proposal*? In the movie, Demi Moore played a wife who, with the support of her husband, decided to have sex with a rich man for a million dollars. After that the couple's marriage fell apart. Was it the affair that broke their bond? Was it the money that tore their relationship apart? Was it the greed both of them experienced? I think it was the greed, their desire to be rich, that led to their brokenness. Think about it: If they hadn't wanted the money so badly, the wife wouldn't have had an affair. And the husband wouldn't have ever asked her to.

No doubt money is easy to worship, especially in the culture we live in. Just consider our fascination with rich people. Sure, throughout history people have been intrigued by wealth. But because of the media [TV shows like *MTV Cribs* and *The Fabulous Life*] and the abundance of wealth and celebrity in our nation, we have for the first time been able to witness life on the *other* side like never before. So it's not just the wealthy who are tempted to worship money; it's us regular folk, too.

Think about your own life; despite our being middle-class, upper-middle-class, or extremely poor, much of our existence revolves around money. Our education, where we live and work, the friends we choose to have or not have, how we spend our free time, the gadgets we'd do almost anything for, and so much more can become influenced—for some of us, controlled—by the institution of money. Because money is such an integral part of our lives—you know, the whole "we need it to survive and not become a burden to society" thing—the line between the *worship* of money and *healthy and godly* thinking about money can get very blurry. However, some people's lines are blurry not because of confusion, but more likely because of a refusal to admit they are consumed by money.

Now, you might be thinking, *Matthew, this is a bunch of crap; I* am not *controlled* or *influenced* that *much by money!* Well, okay. I believe you. However, just keep reading; this book is just getting started. *I totally just dissed you, and you're still reading.* LOSER!

Okay, I take it back.

I said I take it back. You're not a loser.

When it comes to knowing whether or not you worship money, there's really no checklist to follow. Of course, if you've ever literally bowed down to a dollar bill, you might want to just start reading your Bible right now; I can't help you. Well, I guess I could help you, but, you know, sin is contagious, *and I wouldn't want to catch what you have.* However, just like most Christians have differing opinions about baptism, eternal security, and masturbation, they also have *very* different views about the precarious state of "money worship." Seriously, one man's money worship is another man's altar call. [③ Give

that last sentence some time; you'll laugh or think of it as truth — *eventually*.]

Depending on things like our worldview, church denomination, interpretation of the Scriptures, and upbringing, Christians differ greatly in their thinking about what Jesus meant when he said, "You cannot serve both God and Money" (Matthew 6:24, NIV). While some believe Jesus was teaching the importance of pursuing a lifestyle that is poor in spirit, others believe he merely desires us to know and understand that everything we have — whether it's a little or a lot — belongs to him. I think both of these ideas are true; however, I don't think either statement comes close to communicating the weight of Jesus' words.

As you probably know, a person's worship is revealed through every aspect of his or her being. When it comes to our love or lust for money, our true affection is mostly exposed through our actions, thoughts, spiritual posture, goals, habits, and likes and dislikes. Only you and God know whether or not the worship of money is a struggle or temptation for you.

Instead of money being a form of contention between God and us, I believe Jesus wants his followers to utilize money in worship toward him. It's not like I believe he wants us to sacrifice our iPods and BMWs as burnt offerings; however, most Christian scholars do believe that tithing is indeed a form of worship. It seems financial giving or *the offering of possessions* is something that's quite important to God throughout Scripture. I think Jesus taught it best. In the Gospels, he speaks several times about people who were both willing and unwilling to give *all they had* in order to follow him. Consider his praise of the woman who gave only two coins (see Luke 21:1-3). It wasn't the amount of her gift that he was praising; it was her willingness to give all she had to the kingdom. Again in his interaction with the rich young ruler, Jesus asked him to give up everything he had in order to follow him. But the man refused (see Luke 18:18-23).

I often wonder what would have happened if the rich young ruler had been willing to give up his riches and follow Jesus. It seems to me Jesus wasn't so much interested in the man's money as he was with the man's heart.

And that's the key. The condition of your heart tells

The Truth About God and Money

Did you know that the phrase "In God We Trust" hasn't always been printed on U.S. currency? Well, here's the backstory: In 1861, a whole bunch of people were experiencing renewed faith in God [because of the Civil War — go figure]. Because of this revival of sorts, Secretary of Treasury Salmon P. Chase began receiving a number of appeals asking that the U.S. recognize the Deity on its currency. Apparently when Secretary Chase received his first letter [from Reverend M. R. Watkinson, minister of the gospel, from Ridleyville, Pennsylvania],* he thought it was a splendid idea. However, he had no idea that it would require an act of Congress to allow such a change and also that it would take almost three years for the inscription of "In God We Trust" to first appear on the two-cent coin.** After that, Congress continued to pass legislation that approved the printing of the motto on all coins. In 1956, Congress declared "In God We Trust" to be the national motto of the United States and decided it would be printed on all U.S. currency.

Now, Reverend Watkinson believed quite strongly that the recognition of God on U.S. money would indeed be a powerful action, one that would help ensure God's protection of America. Here's an excerpt from his letter to Secretary Chase: "[Recognizing God on U.S. coins] would relieve us from the ignominy [according to Dictionary.com, this word means, "great personal dishonor or humiliation"] of heathenism. This would place us openly under the Divine protection we have personally claimed. From my hearth I have felt our national shame in disowning God as not the least of our present national disasters." This quote can be found on United States Department of the Treasury, "Fact Sheets: Currency & Coins: History of 'In God We Trust,'" http://www.treas.gov/education/fact-sheets/currency/in-god-we-trust.shtml.

**For some reason, in 1883 the motto disappeared from the five-cent coin and, strangely enough, didn't reappear until the Jefferson nickel was created in 1938. Since then, the inscription has appeared on every coin.*

whether or not you worship money, possessions, celebrity, and the like. You can be poor, rich, somewhat wealthy, or somewhat poor and *still* worship money. It's not about how much you have; it's about your heart. I have to be honest; I'm far from rich, but still I wonder what my response to Jesus would be if he were to ask me to give all of my belongings to the poor and follow him. Would I be willing to give up all that I own? I don't know; however, I know I'm not like the woman who gave every last penny to the kingdom. Yet I also know that *her* mentality is how Jesus desires me to think and live.

So think about it: Do you worship *God* or *money*? [It can't be both.]

I'll talk more about the spiritual aspect of money later on in the book.

Six Questions with David Lance

This thirty-one-year-old recovering shopping addict once spent $2,675 on a pair of pants and a shirt. No, that's not a misprint. Here he is answering my six questions!

MPT: You're a shopping addict, right? What exactly does a shopping addict do?

DAVID: [Laughs] It's a person who spends a lot of money shopping compulsively — most of which gets put on a credit card.

MPT: So do you get shopping urges?

DAVID: I used to. Before I began seeking help* for my addiction, I would run to the store every time I saw a commercial for a new watch or cologne I liked, and it was always expensive. I once had thirty-two watches — a different one for every day of the month!

MPT: So what made you decide to get help?

DAVID: I went to a see a counselor at my church about some anxiety I was experiencing. After talking for three or four visits, she asked me how much debt I was in. And at the time, I was just over $19,000 in debt.

Yes, there's professional help for "shopoholism." [🙄 Someone else's word, not mine! If you think you might suffer from compulsive shopping or a shopping addiction, visit Addictions.org for more information.]

MPT: Wow. And all of it was from the addiction — the addiction to go out and shop?

DAVID: I'd say about 95 percent of it was.

MPT: You couldn't have become addicted to Wal-Mart?

DAVID: [Laughs] Umm, no.

MPT: So do you think you worshiped money?

DAVID: If being controlled by something is worship, then yes, I worshiped money. But eventually, God became a part of my recovery. It's still a struggle for me for sure, but I'm learning. My debt is down to about $12,000. . . . I have to pray my way through situations, and I go to see a counselor once a month. Overall, I'm on the mends!

Is 10 Percent the Rule?

[the deal with tithing]

Where in the Bible does it mention the idea of tithing?
Tithing is mentioned several times in the Old Testament. One example is Leviticus 27:30: "A tenth of the produce of the land, whether grain or fruit, belongs to the LORD and must be set apart to him as holy."

The Financial Wisdom of King Solomon

When I was young I used to pray to God asking him for wisdom; however, I was secretly hoping he would bestow upon me riches *and* wisdom — just like he did for King Solomon. Unfortunately, I guess my heart's true motive stuck out like a flashing triple-X sign in the Bible belt. When King Solomon prayed for wisdom, he must have done so with a clean heart because he ended up scoring both wisdom and wealth. Gosh, Solomon was lucky. I mean, *not only* did he manage to become rich and get all the ladies, but God also made him the wisest man in the world. Go figure. Of course, at the end of his life he became depressed and lonely and walked away from God. [Maybe I should take that prayer back.]

However, Solomon's wisdom, as recorded in Proverbs and Ecclesiastes, reveals a lot of truth about money. Consider the following verses in which the richest *and* wisest man in the world speaks of the hardships and frustrations of being loaded.

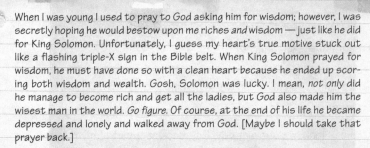

Honor the LORD with your wealth and with the best part of everything your land produces. (Proverbs 3:9)

The wealth of the rich is their fortress; the poverty of the poor is their calamity.
The earnings of the godly enhance their lives, but evil people squander their money on sin. (Proverbs 10:15-16)

Trust in your money and down you go! But the godly flourish like leaves in spring. (Proverbs 11:28)

Wealth from get-rich-quick schemes quickly disappears; wealth from hard work grows. (Proverbs 13:11)

Dishonest money brings grief to the whole family, but those who hate bribes will live. (Proverbs 15:27)

The wise have wealth and luxury, but fools spend whatever they get. (Proverbs 21:20)

A person who makes money by charging interest will lose it. It will end up in the hands of someone who is kind to the poor. (Proverbs 28:8)

What did they tithe during biblical times? Whatever God provided unto them they tithed on, whether it was from farming, herding, or other professions.

Is tithing mentioned in the New Testament? No, but it's not refuted either. And, even though the term *tithing* isn't used, Jesus mentions the act of giving generously to God and his work a lot.

What does the word *tithe* mean? It literally means a *tenth* of a whole.

Does the Bible mention any repercussions if you do not tithe? Many scholars believe Malachi 3:8-9 spells disaster for those who do not tithe. It says,

"Will a man rob God? Yet you rob me.

"But you ask, 'How do we rob you?'

"In tithes and offerings. You are under a curse—the whole nation of you—because you are robbing me." (NIV)

Is ten percent the rule for tithing? Not exactly. Though the Old Testament refers to this percentage as a rule, many preachers believe it's simply a standard, a jumping-off point. As mentioned earlier in this section, Jesus was quite pleased when the widow gave *all* that she had.

Should I tithe off of my gross income or my net income? The Bible isn't clear. It simply says that we should give the *first* tenth of our "fruits."

Will I receive financial blessing if I tithe? Again in Malachi 3, God says, "Bring all the tithes into the storehouse so there will be enough food in my Temple. If you do, . . . I will open the windows of heaven for you. I will pour out a blessing so great you won't have enough room to take it in! Try it! Let me prove it to you!" (verse 10). However, I don't believe this verse implies the "blessing" must be *financial*.

Are there any strange verses in Scripture that refer to tithing? Well, maybe. The King James Version says this in

Deuteronomy 14:22,25-26:

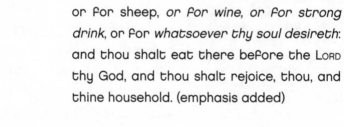

> Thou shalt truly tithe all the increase of thy seed, that the field bringeth forth year by year. . . .
>
> Then shalt thou turn it into money, and bind up the money in thine hand, and shalt go unto the place which the LORD thy God shall choose:
>
> And thou shalt bestow that money for *whatsoever thy soul lusteth* after, for oxen, or for sheep, *or for wine, or for strong drink*, or for *whatsoever thy soul desireth*: and thou shalt eat there before the LORD thy God, and thou shalt rejoice, thou, and thine household. (emphasis added)

Does the Bible mention how our tithe should be used? Yes. Again in Deuteronomy 14:28-29 it says, "At the end of every third year bring the tithe of all your crops and store it in the nearest town. Give it to the Levites, who have no inheritance among you, as well as to the foreigners living among you, the orphans, and the widows in your towns, so they can eat and be satisfied. Then the LORD your God will bless you in all your work."

The Bible Gone Wild?!?

[the story of Ananias and Sapphira]

One of the strangest biblical stories happens in Acts 5:1-11. It's the story of Ananias and his wife, Sapphira. Apparently the pair sold some land and was expected to give the money over to the church. However, instead of giving all of the money to the church, they decided to keep some for themselves. Yeah, this didn't make God very happy; they "mysteriously" died right there on the spot [in front of some other church people]. Needless to say, the people who witnessed this became a bit spooked.

Musings on Church and Money

I have a confession to make. When I was a teenager, I wasn't a big fan of tithing. The thought of giving God 10 percent of my money didn't compute. In my opinion, God didn't need my twenty dollars a week. My church needed it, but God certainly didn't.

My pastor at that time had another point of view. He poured his heart and soul into semiannual "Give God 10 Percent" sermons, ones in which he would yell and scream about the church needing money [he saw the church and God as one and the same]. Conveniently, one of these sermons would happen just in time for the church's yearly budget planning, and the other would occur right before Christmas when "giving" was often known to decline. Like a politician rallying his faithful around a core party issue, my pastor would use every tactic in the book in the hopes of scoring *my* twenty dollars a week.

Sometimes my church would have a month-long fundraising program in which the pastor would encourage the entire congregation to give, give, give. Oftentimes in the back of the church a large red cash-o-meter hung on the wall. Each week the meter, which was basically a large, hand-drawn thermometer, would reveal how close the church was to its financial goal. Sometimes the goal was debt-related, other times it was for a new addition, and once in a great while, it would go toward a particular church ministry. But most often the money collected simply helped the church pay its bills. Usually, despite modest cash flow in the first three weeks, the goal would "miraculously" be met by the time the final Sunday of the program rolled around. It wasn't until I got older that I realized how this actually happened. Either one of the church's rich members would make up the difference *or* a *matching fund* would be set up so that every

Seven Rules a Preacher Should Follow When Talking About Money!

1 Never use the "I didn't want to talk about this, but God asked me to" excuse. We rarely believe it.

2 Take the offering before you begin talking about money. Sorry, but we're overly suspicious.

3 If the money sermon you're preaching is for a particular reason — like the church is in debt or it can't pay its electric bill or you need a vacation — please make this clear up front. We'll respect you more!

4 Nobody likes a beggar! So please don't beg.

5 Speak more about the offering being a type of worship to God, and less about the church's budget needs.

6 Drop the PowerPoint presentation when talking about money; it just feels too corporate to us.

7 Just be honest! If you can't honestly address the subject, you probably shouldn't address it at all.

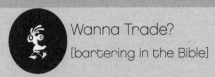

Wanna Trade?
[bartering in the Bible]

Money wasn't *always* used during Bible times, especially in the Old Testament. However, that doesn't mean people like Moses didn't have purchasing power. On the contrary, if Moses had a need — a few sheep, a new pair of sandals, a wife — he didn't pull out his American Express. Instead, he made a trade. Can you imagine hearing someone utter these words: "I'll give you thirty-seven sheep for two of your prettiest daughters"? In the Bible, these kinds of transactions happened all the time! In 1 Kings 5:10-11, we read about a time when King Solomon needed some cedar and cypress wood so he could build a temple. In order to get that kind of wood, Solomon sent 125,000 bushels of wheat and 115,000 gallons of virgin olive oil yearly to feed the king of Tyre's workmen. In return, they provided him timber from the Lebanon forest! So, yeah, during Bible times, trading — *not* Visa — was everywhere you wanted to be. Yep, sometimes the Bible is just plain weird. What can I say?

dollar the church members gave would be matched by the "rich guys." I guess the deacon board offered many thanks that the holy government gives tax deductions; rich people in that church were always looking for deductions.

No matter what church you go to, sermons about money can be a little awkward. It doesn't matter how diplomatic the pastor's words, congregations aren't overly fond of money talks when they're coming from behind a pulpit. Even to some of the most devout followers, sermons on money make parishioners about as comfortable as Lil' Kim in the Catholic Church. I learned this early. Almost every Sunday night when I was a kid, my family and I would watch Jerry Falwell's *Old Time Gospel Hour*. Toward the end of each episode, Jerry would come on and beg the viewing audience for money. This always infuriated my father, not

What Do You Think About Money?
[this chart might help!]

Okay, so you're	You've taken the vow of	You'd do anything	Your idea of luxury is	To you, money worship is	And you	What would Mother Teresa say?
A monk	poverty	for a Big Mac	helping the needy	having some	don't have any	"I can't help it; I think monks are hot!"
A Baptist	tithing	to have special music during the offering	Pontiac, Michigan	giving any-thing less than 10 percent	give 11 percent for good measure	"Bless your little heart."
A World Vision thirty-hour famine participant	short-term poverty	if your friends were going to do it	anything that makes you look good	anything more extrava-gant than Prada	wish you had a closet full of Prada	"Spend a lifetime in India and then call me, kid."
A member of a mega-church	ministerial capitalism [I made up that term]	for Jesus! Heck, you'd work harder if the job he offered paid in cash.	your sweet little spot in suburbia	being consumed by money	think about money a lot, but you are not consumed	"You don't have a clue, honey!"
A CCM artist	telling your audience about World Vision	for a smoke	getting $15K a night to lead worship [yeah, it happens]	Yeah, you try not to think about that too much.	still aren't talking about it	Sorry, Mother Teresa doesn't have any-thing to say about you.
World-renowned Christian author Rick Warren	saving the world	for a little less purpose	raising awareness about Africa	all around us	admit to fighting its evil grip	"Next time, use one of my quotes on the Starbucks cup!"
A preacher in the fastest-growing church in America	preaching, prosperity, and making a lot of money	to make yourself feel good about being you	living your best life now!	No comment	No comment	"True pros-perity is giving your life away for nothing in return."

because Dad didn't believe in giving money to the church, but because every Sunday Jerry made it seem like his ministry was about to go bankrupt. Of course, Jerry was wealthy enough to provide viewers who offered their support a "gift," which was either a bunch of Jerry's preaching tapes, a wall hanging of the Ten Commandments, or a picture of our Founding Fathers with the words "In God We Trust" printed at the bottom.

Perhaps if Jerry had stopped buying so many gifts, he wouldn't have had to spend fifteen minutes every week asking for more money. Hey, it's just a thought. Now, enough with the rambling.

Money Won't Make You Happy— A Podcast Interview with Nate and Thom

[they learned this the hard way]

I realize you're holding a book, but to liven things up a bit, let's pretend this next part of section 1 is a podcast.* Do you mind? Of course you don't mind. Anything to break up the monotony of a book is cool, right? Now, just so you know, you're going to have to use your imagination a

---

*Though this part was not originally a podcast, this interview was recorded. However, parts of the recording have been edited out — because this is a book.

bit. And, yes, I do realize this could be the worst idea I've ever come up with, but, hey, let's at least try it and see what happens. You never know; it might just work. You ready? Here we go.

[Play twenty seconds of *The Apprentice* theme music — "Money, Money, MONEY! **MONEY!**" Now fade.]

MPT: Hi, gang, welcome to another exciting edition of the "*My* Parents Didn't Teach Me Jack" podcast. I'm your host, Matthew Paul Turner. I believe this is going to be an exciting show. Not only are we going to be talking about a very interesting topic — *money* — but we've also got a couple special guests with us today, Nate Baker and Thomas Moreland [names changed]. Of course, I'll be throwing in a few surprises, too. I'm not sure what those surprises will be, but trust me, you'll know them when they occur. Okay, so let me go ahead and introduce our special guests to you fine readers at home. To my right, hailing all the way from Brentwood, Tennessee, we have twenty-six-year-old Thomas Moreland. How you doing, Thom? And that's Thom with an *h*, folks.

THOM: I'm doing good, man.

MPT: Are you sure? You don't sound too good.

THOM: No, I'm good. Just had a little Taco Bell before I came over.

NATE: *Greeaaatt*, that means Thom's gonna be *full* of surprises.

MPT: Well, you better keep your surprises to yourself. [Laughs] Okay, moving right along. To my left, all the way from Franklin, Tennessee, a man who, according to Thom, always seems to have the hookup with the ladies, *Mr. Nate Baker*! You're twenty-five, right?

NATE: Yep.

MPT: So what's going on today, Nate?

NATE: Oh, nothing much.

MPT: You guys live pretty boring lives, huh?

NATE: [Laughs]

THOM: [Laughs] Dude, don't make me laugh — it could get dangerous; my stomach's churning.

[DUE TO THE GRAPHIC NATURE OF THE CONTENT, SEVENTEEN SECONDS OF "AIRTIME" HAVE BEEN EDITED OUT HERE.]

MPT: Now, guys, let me explain to our listening [or reading] audience why I have specifically asked you to be a part of this "podcast." Since this book is about money, I thought it might be interesting to talk to two friends — you guys are friends, right? [Both shake their heads yes.] You have to speak up, guys — they can't hear you shake your heads.

THOM: Yes, we're friends.

NATE: Since eighth grade, maybe it was seventh grade — yeah, it was seventh grade. Cuz I was dating Shannon at the time.

MPT: Thanks, Nate, for reminding the audience you're *not* gay.

NATE: I didn't . . .

MPT: It's okay, man; I was just kidding. Anyway, I wanted to bring Thom and Nate on the show today to talk about money. Though friends, these two guys experienced very different childhoods. But, surprisingly, as you'll hear [or read], those experiences have led to very similar challenges regarding the financial problems they have faced. That pretty much explains where we're going with this, right?

NATE: Umm, I think so, Matthew *Paul* Turner [said in fake radio voice].

THOM: [Laughs] Dude, why *do you use* your middle name? I always knew you as Matthew Turner until you became this big-time author dude.

MPT: Well, the short story is this: There's a famous cellist and a famous chess player who are both named Matthew Turner. And I didn't want to have to compete with them for Google space. Yeah, I know, *vain*.

NATE and THOM: [Laugh]

[DUE TO THE GRAPHIC NATURE OF THE CONTENT, THIRTY-TWO SECONDS OF "AIRTIME" HAVE BEEN EDITED OUT HERE.]

MPT: Okay, guys, we're wasting time. As I was explaining, you two come from *very* different financial backgrounds. Thom, why don't we start with you? Tell us a little about your childhood.

THOM: Well, I was born here in Nashville — a pretty poor area of Nashville. My mom was a single mother of two [Thom has an older brother]. My dad left my mom shortly after I was born, which meant she had to work two jobs. . . . Not only did I not have a father, but I also rarely saw my mother.

MPT: Thom, can you explain to the audience what you mean by poor?

THOM: Well, it wasn't exactly *poverty*, but we constantly struggled. Mom rented this dinky four-room apartment furnished with other people's junk. I remember one time my mom coming home very excited. Our neighbors had decided to get rid of their kids' bunk bed — Mom snatched that bed from beside the dumpster.

MPT: Did you end up using the bed?

THOM: Heck, yeah; my brother and I thought that thing was *sweet*. It stunk like trash at first, but that eventually faded.

MPT: What were Christmases like for you growing up?

THOM: Depressing. We had one of those awful *glass* Christmas trees — it was like eighteen inches high, and it had a light bulb inside of it. . . .

MPT and NATE: [both of us give Thom a confused look]

THOM: You guys have never seen a glass Christmas tree?

NATE: Umm, *no*.

THOM: Well, they exist — we *had* one. But anyway, my brother and I each got a gift or two. But that was it. Some years my grandmother would give us twenty dollars each. But I remember a couple of times Mom ended up using that to pay bills.

MPT: Thom, thank you for sharing your story; I know it's probably not easy.

THOM: No, it's okay.

MPT: Nate, your story is rather different from Thom's; tell us about your childhood.

NATE: Well, I was raised in Nashville, too. Yeah, I had it easy — *very* easy. Dad's a doctor, Mom is a Realtor, and my family was very well off. We weren't living like *Bill Gates*, but my parents spoiled us a lot. This might be a little of an exaggeration, but seriously, almost everything I wanted, my parents would go out and buy for me. Back then I thought it was great, but now I look back and think it was completely ridiculous.

MPT: Okay, so how did your past affect you later in life?

NATE: I was an idiot with money. When I went away to college, I used my parents' money as a way to get friends, keep friends, manipulate friends. Whatever I wanted, I would go out and buy it. It got very ugly. Every time I ran my credit card up, my parents would bail me out. *Until* I got out of college; then I was on my own. At twenty-three, my credit card debt was over $5K.

MPT: And your parents wouldn't pay it?

NATE: Nope, they refused to, which ended up being the best thing that ever happened to me.

MPT: Okay, hold that thought. Thom, how about you?

THOM: Crazy enough, my story is similar to Nate's. [Laughs] Except my mom wasn't able to bail me out. Man, I never had anything when I was a kid. So when I was out on my own with a job, school, and a credit card, I started living it up. For once in my life, I wanted to "own" something, and I thought things would make me happy. Over time the debt kept rising. Sooner or later, I was in a hole and very unhappy. But, hey, I had an iPod.

MPT: How bad was it — the debt, that is?

THOM: Oh, bro, I'm embarrassed to say. My debt would make Nate's debt seem tame.

MPT: Okay, so you both got into some pretty serious credit card debt during college. . . .

NATE: But, man, you see, the debt isn't the *real* problem. For me, how I thought about money was the problem. It controlled me. I thought money made me happy.

MPT: What finally changed your perspective?

NATE: I think both of us realized God had a purpose for money, and it wasn't about making people happy.

THOM: I didn't really come into my faith until I was out of college. A few months later, my church ended up having a Bible study on money, and I realized that much of my life was being spent looking for personal contentment and joy from money.

NATE: I suppose this was your point in getting us together, Matthew, but isn't it funny how Thomas and I came from two very different backgrounds — wealth versus hardship — yet both of us fell into a lifestyle where money controlled us, became our focus in pursuing happiness? It's not as much about how one was raised as it is how he or she thinks about money.

MPT: Last question, guys: How do you pursue thinking about money now? In other words, for those listening [or reading], what's the core value here that might help them pursue a healthier perspective of money?

THOM: I think it's about realizing that God is the owner of what we have; the truth I want to live is this: to pursue wisdom and generosity in how I utilize what he's given to me.

NATE: Yeah, I think Thom hit it. Before you can get out of debt, before you can make a budget and do all of those other financial things people tell you to do, you first have to pursue the mind-set that God owns what you have. And secondly, money and the stuff that money can buy don't make you happy.

MPT: Thanks, guys, for sharing your stories and wisdom with us; this has been great.

[END OF PODCAST]

Umm, But Can Money Really Not Make You Happy?

According to a 2006 study by Pew Research Center, 49 percent of those who made more than $100K a year considered themselves happy. The same study found that only 24 percent of those making under $30K a year considered themselves happy.[1] [Well, that's cool and all, but it seems to me there's still an awful lot of unhappiness going on in the world — whether you're "poor" or "rich."]

Stewardship: Laying a Foundation That Begins with the Heart

[an interview with David Briggs, director of financial ministry at Willow Creek Church]

If you had told me that an interview with the director of financial ministry at Willow Creek Church — you know, the church with the great drama department and more money than Oprah — was going to be an important part of this book, I would have laughed and had a few sarcastic words to offer. It's not that I don't like Willow Creek; I'm sure it's a fine church. I just thought that a *church* guy would have nothing new to say. However, after my conversation with Mr. Briggs, I became one of his biggest fans. His words about money were inspiring. And his teaching and understanding about what Jesus teaches about money was refreshing [to say the least].

My interview begins here [leading us into section 2] and will conclude toward the end of this book.

MPT: First of all, you've been working around money — in both the corporate and ministry worlds — for more than twenty years. Do you like talking about money?

DAVID: It's been a fascinating topic to think about and discuss from a biblical perspective all these years. Matthew, do you know there isn't a day that goes by when I don't learn something new about human nature and how we deal with issues we're not comfortable talking about? There's no bottom to the well in terms of ever having this topic figured out.

MPT: How did you begin talking about money as a ministry?

DAVID: While I was working at General Electric as a finance manager — a little more than twenty years ago — I received a definitive calling from God that he had a mission for me to find everything in the Bible regarding money and look for practical ways people could change the way they view money and the way they live. I believe God thought that my coming from a businessman's perspective would be unique because I would be coming at the subject without an agenda, not asking for money and not building anything. When you're not reaching into somebody's pockets, they know you're simply there to help them understand some very important biblical truths. So being a businessman, I was able to open up doors that a preacher or someone in ministry couldn't.

MPT: Now that you're working full-time at Willow Creek Church, what is your responsibility?

DAVID: This is a teaching ministry, Matthew. Until people grab hold of this with their heads and hearts and emotions and make a connection that this really is a key part of our relationship with God, then all of the financial mechanics and counseling and all the other stuff has no foundation to rest on. And frankly, until you have that biblical foundation, all the other stuff is rather pointless. So more than anything I am a foundation layer to help people think differently and relate differently to money. And hopefully once people see the relationship between their thinking about money and their relationship with God, they're able to begin budgeting, planning, giving, saving, and investing. Knowing how God thinks about these things will help you establish *why* you should care about these matters. Unfortunately, other Christian financial organizations tend to jump right into the planning, investing, and saving before they've discussed the biblical foundation of money.

MPT: Okay, so, David, why should we care about money?

DAVID: Well, that is the *$64,000* question. We should care because God cares. We should care because God has told us in his Word that if we have a wrong relationship to money, we will have a wrong relationship to him. If we don't get the money thing right, we'll fail to get the God thing right.

Now, that's not just my opinion. When you go through the Bible and see what Jesus said about money and what God said about money, it wasn't about *the money*. It was always about what money did — positively and/or negatively — to humanity's communion with God and Christ.

MPT: For some reason, I think we as people make the money thing too personal. So many of us concentrate on how money is going to affect us, specifically how it's going to affect our futures. Rarely do we think about how it's going to affect what God is doing or how we can use it to help others. Do you agree?

DAVID: Absolutely. And you know, Matthew, it starts with a wrong thinking about money. Part of it is our fault, but I also think it's the fault of the greater Christian community because we're not teaching it, and when we do teach it, we're not teaching the right things. We focus too much on teaching about our "obligation to support God's work." You know, it's the whole "if you belong to the church, you ought to be supporting a church." We teach a lot of the mechanics and the obligations, but most of the time, we miss the whole point about what Christ taught and what the Bible says. We just brush right over most of the teaching about money and possessions. And that combination of not teaching and ineffective teaching fosters a lot of the tug-of-war over money — that place where we begin to take money so personally rather than seeing it as a very important aspect of serving the kingdom.

MPT: Now, David, I know you talk a lot about stewardship in your teachings. Can you give your definition of stewardship?

DAVID: Well, I like to start all conversations about money from the Bible's perspective. And when you read about what a steward was in biblical times, he was an individual who was *always* trusted. This individual had earned the confidence of the master, so much so that the master could, in fact, trust his entire financial livelihood over to the steward. And the steward would always act in the best interest of the master. This relationship was very synergistic; the steward would make a decision exactly like he believed the *master* would make a decision.

Stewardship is living as a biblical steward. Today that means taking what the Master has entrusted to you and handling it the way you believe he would handle it.

MPT: So when you're teaching stewardship, what's the first step?

DAVID: Well, the first thing I do when I'm discussing this topic in a group setting or one-on-one is address this question: Are you living as an *owner* or a *steward*? I bring up two biblical passages in this discussion: the story of Job and the story of the rich young ruler. In the first chapter of Job, it says that he was the richest man in the East; he was God-fearing and upright. But because of a discussion that God and Satan had, God allowed Satan to take all of Job's earthly possessions away. Of course, Satan was convinced that if God were to take Job's possessions away, Job would curse God. So Satan took everything away from Job [including his family]. But how did Job respond? He responded as that of a steward. He said, "You know, I came into this world with nothing. And God has chosen to give me a whole lot, and then he's chosen to take it away, but he's still God." What I love about Job is that despite losing his family and all of his possessions, he never once questioned God's right to give and take away at his discretion. And the Bible says that Job didn't charge God with unfairness, which to me is a perfect example of what it looks like when a steward responds from a proper understanding of God's thinking about money. God gives it. God takes it away. Blessed be the name of the Lord.

Now, the rich young ruler went up to Jesus in Matthew 19 and said, "What must I do to gain eternal life?" Jesus first questioned him about the commandments. And the ruler said, "Well, I've kept all of the commandments since I was a little kid." Then Jesus presented to him one more test. He told him to get rid of all of his stuff and come and follow him. It was at that point the rich young ruler turned and walked away sad because he owned a lot of stuff. He was an *owner* who, when faced with the decision to follow Jesus, was so attached to his stuff — the sense of ownership was so strong — that he gave up the chance of a lifetime to follow the God of the universe.

Again, when I'm talking about money, my question is always, "Are you living like a steward, or are you living like an owner?" Because if you live like an owner, that will forever be a barrier between you and God. Owners have broken relationships with God. If you live like that of steward, you will be able to weather any kind of prosperity or poverty because a steward trusts the Master, who owns it all anyway.

MPT: How does *making* money fit into the concept of stewardship?

DAVID: Well, the Bible does talk about the concept of working and working hard. In Deuteronomy it talks about how God has given us the ability to work and make money. I think a steward works hard, but he works hard while understanding *who* gave him the skills and abilities. The Bible teaches us that when we work, we should do so as though we are working for God. There's nothing in the Bible that says it's wrong to make money, Matthew. But what it always comes down to is this: What is the attitude behind *why* you're doing what you do? Are you desiring to partner with God, to come alongside of him and be passionate about the things he is passionate about? Well, then, that's great; do that. But if you're only working hard to accumulate more stuff so you can build bigger barns and hoard more things, then you are falling into a trap that is going to be incredibly dangerous to your soul and to the relationship you have with God.

MPT: So like most things, it comes back to the condition of our hearts.

DAVID: No question about it. What I have found over the years is that we as Christians get caught up in the *act*, whereas the Bible consistently talks about the attitude. In other words, it's about our hearts. Jesus wasn't interested in the *doing*; he was all about the *why* behind the doing. That was the only thing Christ ever zeroed in on — our motivation, our attitude, and our hearts.

[MY INTERVIEW WITH DAVID BRIGGS WILL CONTINUE LATER IN THIS BOOK.]

Solomon's Big Questions

King Solomon asked a lot of questions in Proverbs. I'm not sure if these questions were meant to be rhetorical or not, but I thought his question about money in Proverbs 17:16 deserved an answer! Here's the question:

Of what use is money in the hand of a fool,
        since he has no desire to get wisdom? (NIV)

Well, Solomon, here's the deal. We foolish people in the twenty-first century have LOTS of ways to use money. We get involved in pyramid schemes! We buy expensive brand names like Versace and FCUK [☺ stands for French Connection, United Kingdom, not a misspelled dirty word]! Some of us even have cars [which are WAY cooler than your chariots] that are worth more than our homes! So today, unlike back when you were alive, the lifestyles of fools who also happen to have money are quite extravagant and limitless. Of course, I realize that was probably your point, but just in case it wasn't, I thought you might want to know a few ways we fools use money. Hope that helps, KS!

**STEWARD:
one who manages
another's property,
finances, or other affairs[2]**

Money Basics
You Need to Know!

The safe way to double
your money is to fold
it over once and put it
in your pocket.

— Frank Hubbard

Back when I sold chicken eggs to the church ladies [okay, can we stop for a moment and consider what I just said?], I would bring my money home and store it inside a metal safety box that I kept under my bed. Whenever I had more than one hundred dollars, my father insisted I give ten dollars to God and put the rest in the bank [more about the bank later].

"That's what you're supposed to do with money," he'd say to me. "You have to give 10 percent to God and save the rest, and when you get five hundred dollars we'll get a special bank account for you."

At first, I often begged to use my money toward something I wanted. But Dad was persistent; that money was for God and college, not some silly toy I'd end up tossing in the Goodwill bag at church six months later.

Like I said, when I was a kid I always tried to buck the proper way of handling money for something a little more free and perhaps a little more about me.

This section is about the proper way to handle money. However, this section is pointless unless one "gets" section 1's final thoughts. Healthy and godly financial living begins with direction of heart and mind. Like Mr. Briggs taught us, before we can take a first step toward a God-centered financial mindset, we must first understand and embrace the idea that we're not *owners* but instead *stewards* of what God has given to us.

Now, in order for us to be good stewards, we must be aware of a few things. The next couple of sections will outline a few basics you need to know so you can be better equipped to pursue a healthy and godly financial lifestyle.

Okay, so first, take a deep breath! This section won't be hard—it may be *a bit boring* at times, but not difficult. So don't worry. This section is just about the basics. Now, are you ready to learn/review/re-review some important [yet basic] stuff about money?

 **LET'S GET STARTED.**

Budgeting!

[bet you haven't heard about this before]

You're rolling your eyes right now, aren't you? Oh, I know you are. You're thinking to yourself, *Oh, Matthew, please tell us something we don't already know about the importance of budgeting!*

See? I'm right, aren't I?

Budgeting talks aren't cool. But when you're talking about money, they're necessary. And for most of you, *your* method of living week to week is clearly not getting you very far.

Most of you have heard all the reasons a budget is important. I've heard the same reasons. But despite all of us *knowing* the importance of a budget, most statistics reveal that few of us take the advice and actually create a financial plan.

Of course, I know why we resist making the effort of financial planning.

No emergency.

No worries.

No discipline.

In other words, you think that because you're making good money, paying all of your bills, and giving the church 10 percent, a budget is not needed. *At least that's how a lot of us think!* Sadly, most of us don't begin doing a budget until we're in the middle of a financial crisis [and some of us resist it even then]. Sure, when the cash is flowing like beer at a frat party, we don't feel the need to worry about comparing our incoming revenue with our expenses, which, I should add, helps us proactively plan for the future, potential *emergencies*, and intentional giving.

But that kind of thinking is incorrect. You NEED a budget. Your biggest obstacle will be your lack of discipline. When it comes to money, *discipline* is such a needed trait. More often than not, it's our lack of discipline that keeps us from beginning a budget or remaining on a budget! So please, try to get past it, and just do it; make a budget. It's not as complicated as you might think, and you'll learn a lot in the process. Keep reading, and I will tell you when it's time to create a budget.

 YOU'RE GOING TO DO IT, RIGHT?

Pretty please?

[Just keep reading.]

Good Reasons You Should Create a Budget

- A budget allows you to see whether or not you're going in the right direction financially.
- A budget puts you in control of your money, instead of allowing your money to control you.
- A budget can help you meet your financial goals — savings, giving, paying off debt, and even vacations.
- A budget can help you plan for big expenses like buying a car, computer, or other pricey possessions.
- A budget can help keep you *out* of debt.
- A budget can help you know how much you're able to give toward charitable organizations and ministries.
- A budget can help you *never* spend more than you make.

Your goal in creating a budget is to learn how you're spending your money. When you know where your hard-earned money is going, you are able to make decisions that will positively affect your financial lifestyle.

However, you might have goals of your own. Perhaps you want to put 10 percent of your income in a savings account. Maybe you'd like to increase your tithe to 15 percent instead of 10. Whatever financial goals you have, making them happen usually begins with a budget, because if you don't know how you're spending your money, how can you possibly know how much you can save? See how simple this is? It's like watching *Blue's Clues*.

An Easy Budgeting Process!

[ONLY five steps]

1 Don't complicate things. The worst thing you can do for yourself [especially if you're ADHD like me] is overthink your budget. Keep things simple! If you don't, you're apt to become overwhelmed and not follow through. And you don't want to do that!

2 Gather one month's worth of financial information. For most, this will be the hardest part of the process [because of the time it takes to do all of this!]. So collect the following items: [HINT: You probably get these items in the mail.]

▤ Bank statements [For most of you, this will be your checking—which includes your check card purchases—and savings accounts statements. If you bank online, you can get this info that way.]

- Monthly bills [Yeah, this includes that brief addiction to that "adult" website you paid to view. You thought I didn't know, didn't you? *I know everything. I just do.*]

- Pay stubs [Eh, basically just know how much you bring home in a month — *post* the IRS getting its share, of course.]

3 **Separate your expenses into categories.** First put all of your monthly bills into categories such as housing, food, insurance, entertainment, etc. [You can be as broad or as specific as you want to be!] Then look over your bank statement and separate all of your check card purchases into your categories.

4 **Add up all of your expenses.** This should be simple. Add up each bill and check card purchase; your sum will be your monthly expense total.

5 **Compare your monthly expense total to your total monthly income.** Of course, this is the moment of truth. If your expenses are lower than your income total, you're in the black. However, if your expenses are higher, you're going to need to make some cuts and adjustments for the future.

FYI: You should probably repeat this process the following month as well to make sure you didn't miss anything or if you believe your expenses were unusually high.

After You Budget

[a few questions to ask yourself!]

○ **Were there any surprises?** When you do a budget for the first time, there's usually something shocking. Perhaps it's that you spent over three hundred dollars on eating out or that you didn't have enough money to tithe. It might be that you have a lot more cash left over than you thought! [However, that happens almost as often as Halley's comet. *Yep, that last line is called random bad humor. It happens.*]

○ **Is there any way to remedy the shock?** Look for ways to fix or make the most of that surprise.

○ **If you have debt, are you just making the payment, or are you proactively trying to get rid of it?** I'll be talking more about this in another section. *Maybe you should begin being proactive before you read that section. It might make you feel better once you get there!*

○ **How much money are you saving?** Most financial experts suggest you should be saving somewhere between 10 to 20 percent of your income. If you're putting your "savings" toward debt, that counts!

○ **Can you give more away?** Sometimes a budget lets us see that we're able to give more to charities, ministries, and other goodwill organizations.

10 You're lazy. And you're not offended that I just called you lazy.

9 *Grey's Anatomy* is on!

8 You get anxious thinking about your financial situation.

7 You don't really care about money. *You're lying. And you're not offended that I just said you're lying.*

6 You're single and you make over $50K a year — you think you're fine!

5 Can you believe it? *Grey's Anatomy* is on — *again!*

4 You believe God will work it all out.

3 "Matthew, would Donald Miller sit around and worry about money?" [Good point! Of course, he sold half a million copies of *Blue Like Jazz*.]

2 You think not knowing about your financial situation is like therapy.

1 Your first name is Pat, Bennie, or Joel [and by darn, you're feeling blessed!].

So will you budget? Or are you just going to read this book with that blank look on your face? *I'm not sure this writer/reader relationship can continue. How can I communicate with you when you won't listen? It's my fault, isn't it?*

[If you're one of the "good people" who actually did do (or already do) a budget, this message is for you!]

 KEEP YOUR BUDGET AND THE DOCUMENTS USED TO MAKE YOUR BUDGET HANDY — WE'LL BE USING THEM A BIT MORE LATER ON IN THIS BOOK!

The Bank and Why It's Your Friend
[well, sometimes]

Have you ever wondered why all banks smell the same? I have. Seriously, almost every bank I have ever walked into smells like a mixture of money, cedar, and generic cleaning supplies. Is it bad that I like that smell? When I was a kid, I wanted to become a bank teller when I grew up, partly so I could sniff that scent all day long. Of course, I also liked that bank tellers used calculators with cool pull bars like slot machines. *And* they got to use red-ink pens. When I was a kid, I *loved* red-ink pens.

When I was ten, my father took me to Union Trust Bank so I could open up a certificate of deposit account. I was so excited I could hardly sleep the night before. I didn't care so much that I was going to be earning 8.2 percent interest on my money [the Reagan years were good for CDs]; I was excited because my father told me that I would have to sign my name on important papers. That would be a first for me. Never before had I signed a document that required me to push down hard on the paper so that my signature would penetrate through each of the four carbon copies. [I had a strange love for signing my name, but that's something I can talk about at another time.]

Now, unless you live in a place like rural Nebraska, banks don't usually use those old carbon forms anymore. No doubt the way we bank has changed quite significantly in the last few years. More than likely, you probably know something about how banking works. But simply knowing that a bank is the place that holds all your money is not enough. Anyone can know how to make deposits, take withdrawals, and avoid overdraft charges [although we do tend to suck at that]. *Yes*, I'm going to tell you other things you need to know about the bank.

I bet you're excited. I certainly am — *not*! [I realize using *not* — as if it is a sentence all by itself — is *a little 1992*, but I am totally acknowledging my flaw, so that makes the uncool cool again . . . right? I think I've heard that rule before.]

Okay, so here are a few things you need to know and do when it comes to banking.

Bank me BABY one more time! [😄 Ha ha ha ha! That was funny. Well, at least it was funny when I wrote it.]

Know the services that banks offer. Most banks offer the following "products." But don't take my word for it; you should check with your bank to see what they can offer you. You might be pleasantly surprised, or you could be disappointed. I guess it depends on what you're looking for and where you're looking.

- Checking and savings accounts [➤ so you don't have to keep cash hidden under the mattress]
- Mortgage loans [➤ so you're able to afford a house, condo, or townhome—or at least *think* you're able to afford it]
- ATMs [➤ to access your money at like a billion locations worldwide]
- Money market accounts [➤ savings accounts that offer higher interest rates in return for *bigger* than normal deposits. However, watch out for the restrictions—they can be heavy.]
- Loan products [➤ so you think you're able to afford a car, expensive band equipment, and other large-ticket items. Yes, *this is debt!*]
- Credit cards [➤ I have a feeling you know what these are for. We'll talk about them later.]
- Brokerage services [➤ so a friend can help you play the stock market, make a ton of money, and then purchase a

really hot car. Banks can provide these "friends."]

- ⚏ Online banking services [➤ so you can pay your bills while sitting on the toilet. Of course, you'll need a laptop and wireless service to do this. And if you live in a small town, this service might not be available.]

- ⚏ Check cards [➤ looks like a Visa, spends like a check: one of the best inventions of the twentieth century]

When you're choosing a bank, shop around. While you're in college, any bank that offers free checking and a check card might do, but once you're out of school and have a job, you might want to shop around to see which bank will work best for your financial needs. Good banks are prepared to fight for new customers, so don't just pick the first bank you walk into. When visiting banks, compare interest rates, all the potential [usually petty] fees, and all the services I just mentioned in the last point. If you're too busy to shop, you might consider hiring a financial agent who has a relationship with several banks; he or she, although pricey, will be able to advise you on your best option. [EXTRA: Some banks, especially when you're able to keep more than one thousand dollars in your account at all times, will waive ATM and other petty fees. And believe me, those one- to three-dollar fees add up over time!]

Get to know the folks at your bank. With the invention of ATMs, online banking, and check cards, it's now rare to have an actual relationship with a person at a bank. But relationships with the people at your bank are important. When you and your bankers have a relationship, you're apt to get the best interest rates on loans and savings accounts. And you might get a lollipop, too. [If you live in a large city where banks

ATMs Equal $$$

In the United States alone, ATM fees add up to two billion dollars in revenue each year for banks.[3] Think about that the next time you agree to pay the extra fee.

have locations everywhere, choose one convenient location and on occasion do your business inside rather than at the drive-through or ATM.]

Two More Things for Extra Credit
[just because we're getting along so well]

Open an online savings account. Why? Not only are sites like etrade.com and ing-usa.com easy to use, but they also offer higher interest rates than regular banks do. Just make sure the online bank you use is protected by the FDIC.* And avoid using foreign banks! Unless you're a finance expert, foreign banks can be hard to read.

---

* *This is one of those acronyms that everyone mentions, but few people know what each letter stands for. Well, now you do: Federal Deposit Insurance Corporation [umm, this government-run agency insures your bank deposits up to $100,000].*

- ⊞ **Ask your bank if you're getting the best deal.** [Whether you're opening a checking account, getting a loan, or applying for a credit card, *always* ask if you're getting the best deal.]

- ⊞ **If your place of employment has it, use direct deposit.** Banks often offer better deals with DD. You might get free checking, a higher yield on savings, or a free bank teddy bear. And you avoid the hassle of having to take your check to the bank every other Friday.

- ⊞ **If your bank offers online banking, use it.** Keep track of your accounts, pay your bills, and set up automatic payments for your monthly bills. On most banks' websites, these functions are all very easy to do. [Of course, *only* do automatic bill pay if you know you're going to have the funds.]

- ⊞ **Don't be afraid to ask for a break.** If you're a first-time "check bouncer" [heck, even if you were once a chronic check bouncer but it's been awhile since it happened], go to the bank [in person] and explain your situation; if you're nice about it, they might surprise you with a little bank mercy. [😊 A few tears of desperation can't hurt.]

- ⊞ **Paper, please, and . . .** I know we're living in the digital age where bank statements are available online, and I'm sure this technology saves a few trees [and, of course, saves the bank a *ton* of $ $ $]. But you're apt to forget to look at your statement if it's online. So when the bank asks, "Paper or digital?" choose both! No, seriously, choose both. *BOTH!* [Yes, I'm yelling, but I'm not really sure why.]

▧ **Your bank should provide it free of charge.** [Unless you've got money to burn, you should never pay for it.]

▧ **Ask your bank if they provide free bill pay.** [This allows you to pay all of your bills via the Internet.]

▧ **Do not print your social security number on your personal checks.** [Why? Identity theft.] In fact, it's recommended that you don't print your phone number on your personal checks either. [Personal information should be protected. Because personal-check technology has improved, merchants should not need an overabundance of personal information. And if they do, you can write the information on the check for them.]

▧ **Make sure you record all check-card purchases.** Keep all of your receipts and do this at least once a week. [Some people use their credit card as their only purchasing tool and pay it off every month with their checking account. Of course, you have to be überdisciplined to do this, so I don't recommend it for anyone except you crazy organized legalists. But either way, you'll need to keep track of your purchases.]

▧ **Carefully review your account statement each month to ensure that your record keeping matches that of the bank.** [Well, if you think all merchants, banks, and credit card companies are honest, then by all means ignore this point so you'll avoid wasting your time.]

▧ **Ask your bank if they offer a checking account with interest.** [For those of you able to keep your accounts above five hundred to one thousand dollars, you have a decent chance of scoring a few extra bucks a year.]

▧ **Know your account's limitations and fees.** [Some banks charge a ridiculous number of fees for a various number of reasons, including use of non-branch ATMs, going over a set number of deposits each month, non-ATM deposits, debit card use at grocery stores and gas stations, and more. So read the fine print of your account's contract or talk to your bank!]

The Editors of What You Didn't Learn from Your Parents About Money Talk About Social Security

Hey, dearie! It's the editors! You'll hear a lot more from us a little later, but first, let's answer some of the basic questions you need to know about Social Security!

Definition? Well, honey, according to investorguide.com, Social Security is defined as "the comprehensive federal program of benefits providing workers and their dependents with retirement income, disability income, and other payments."[5] Ha ha! But, baby, unless there's some major reform on how the government handles Social Security, some people think it's gonna go bye-bye!

How does Social Security get funded? You! It comes out of your paycheck. A small Social Security tax [called FICA on your pay stub] is taken out of your paycheck by your

Avoid borrowing money from a bank. Why? According to Tax Matters' online office, sometimes a bank is the last place you should borrow money from.[4] Find out if the *seller* offers financing on the item you're buying. Many times you can save 2 to 5 percent on interest rates *or* get a short-term loan with no interest for six to twelve months. [EXTRA: You might also check to see if a family member would help you out.]

A Few Money-Related Terms You Should Know

Okay, so we've learned a few basics together, but we're not quite finished. It's now time to get familiar with a few of those confusing financial terms that smart people use when they're trying to sound economically intelligent.

- **Asset.** This one is easy; an asset is something you own. It can be anything from land to a building to a diamond ring to equipment — even cash. No, body parts do not count. **EXTRA:** Your assets minus your liabilities equal your personal net worth. [You'll learn about liabilities in a second. And, umm, no, it's not a weight-loss drug.]

- **Cash flow.** This is how much money comes into your home [income, interest, etc.] and how much goes out [bills, debt, etc.]. You know how money is! It flows in and flows out!

- **Audit.** Perhaps one of the scariest words in the human language, an audit is when the IRS reviews your tax return and asks you to prove that you correctly reported your income and deductions.

employer. It's also fun to say, *What the FICA are you talking about?* Hee hee.

How long has it been around? Since 1935. You can thank FDR [he was one of our presidents, dumb dumb] for this one!

When am I eligible for coverage? The current qualifying age is sixty-five. So you've got a long time to wait! [Plus, a person must work ten years earning at least $3,120 each year.]

Will I earn enough from SS to retire? Ha ha ha ha ha! That question makes us laugh. No, baby, probably not. It should only be considered a supplemental income for retirement.

How can I find out more information? Visit www.socialsecurity .gov or call 1-800-772-1213.

Tootles for now!

>>The editors

PS: Write us! Our e-mail is WeLoveWritingForMatthew@ yahoo.com.

- **Bond.** An interest-bearing security that contractually binds the issuer [or person/company offering the bond] to pay a specific percentage of interest for a determined time, usually three to seven years, and then repay the bondholder the original amount of the bond. In other words, you give a company five thousand dollars for five years, they pay you 8 percent interest to use your money for five years, and then at the end of five years, you get your money back. [At least that's how it's supposed to work.]

- **Term insurance.** Insurance that guarantees you a particular amount of money [if you were to die] for a fixed amount of time.

- **Mortgage equity.** In simple terms, it means "ownership." So let's say you've paid $25,000 on the mortgage of your home, plus your home's value has appreciated by $16,000. Your accumulated equity [or ownership] would be $41,000.

- **Home equity loans.** You know that $41,000 of *equity* we just talked about? Well, a home equity loan allows you to borrow money against that amount. **EXTRA:** This transaction is sometimes called a second mortgage.

- **Premium.** The cost of an insurance policy.

- **401k.** A company-sponsored retirement plan that lets employees put pretaxed dollars into an investment plan. Sometimes companies will match an employee's contribution up to a certain amount. Your money remains tax free until you withdraw the funds or roll them into another pretaxed retirement plan.

- **Junk bond.** A risky, high-yield bond (see above) rated "BB" or lower by Standard & Poor's. These bonds are usually offered by unknown or financially weak companies, or they have only limited backing.

- **Liability.** Anything you've purchased and are still paying for is a liability. [That new "friend" of yours might be a liability, too.]

- **Points.** According to Kiplinger.com, points are important to know because "points paid on a mortgage to buy or improve your principal residence are generally fully deductible in the year you pay them. You even get to deduct points paid for you by the seller of the home. Points paid to refinance the mortgage on a principal home or to buy any other property must be deducted over the life of the loan."[6] When you're buying a home, each point is equal to 1 percent of the mortgage amount.

- **Prime rate.** Yeah, so if you're a bank's best customer, you get their best rate!

- **Depreciation.** A big word to describe a gradual loss of value on an asset. **EXTRA:** Depreciation is relevant mostly for tax purposes—it allows you to deduct an asset from your taxes [you know, a tax break over a period of a few years rather than all at once].

Now, I promise that the rest of this book won't jump around quite so much as the first part did. It will jump around some; it just won't give you literary whiplash. Will you forgive me?

I'll give you five dollars.

Okay, so I probably won't. I'm lying.
But will you still forgive me? PLEASE?

Now on to section 3.

 By the Numbers: U.S. Currency

* **37,000,000:** Number of currency notes made by the BEP [Bureau of Engraving and Printing] each day, according to the U.S. Treasury Department
* **$698,000,000:** Face value of the 37,000,000 currency notes made each day by the BEP
* **.00043:** Thickness of U.S. currency notes in inches
* **1:** Weight of a dollar bill in grams
* **95:** Percentage of the BEP's yearly currency printing said to be replacing money already in circulation
* **18:** Average circulation life in months of a one-dollar bill
* **2,040.8:** Weight in pounds of $1,000,000 distributed in one-dollar bills[7]

Spending and Saving

[how the two can work together]

> When you've got [people] by their wallets, their hearts and minds will follow.
>
> — Fern Naito

Do you agree with Fern's quote? I once worked for a man who definitely agreed. As a fundraiser for a ministry, my friend believed it wasn't enough for an individual church to simply *say* it was behind his ministry; he wanted them to *show* it. And to him, that was revealed in whether or not they chose to give money toward the ministry. He often told me, "Just getting on to a budget of a church almost always makes them more interested in the ministry. It's crazy, Matthew, but money leads our emotions and our will and says what we're truly passionate about."

And although in certain situations this may be arguable, most of us would find it hard to deny that there is a lot of truth to Fern's words. Before writing this book, I knew money could be powerful and that it influenced our lives to a great extent. But I don't think I knew exactly how much. In talking with so many spiritual leaders, especially those who study and work in finance, I've been awakened to how our financial habits truly show where our passion lies.

Now, looking at our financial habits is certainly not the only way to test our passions, but it's a good one. How we handle money is very much a foreshadowing of the rest of our lives. I'm quite sure some of you think that all of this is gibberish [and, umm, I must admit I've been there a time or two myself]; you believe that where you put *and don't put* your money say very little about the condition of your heart. Well, I've thought that, too. But honestly, I'm pretty aware of how gross my heart can be at times. I naturally gravitate toward being selfish. I LOVE thinking about me, especially when it comes to money. You know how it is, right? Well, let me be a real pain in the butt and just remind both you and me of what Jesus said:

> "Do not store up for yourselves treasures on earth, where moth and rust destroy, and where thieves break in and steal. But store up for yourselves treasures in heaven, where moth and rust do not destroy, and where thieves do not break in and steal. For where your treasure is, there your heart will be also." (Matthew 6:19-21, NIV)

So do you *still* believe that how you spend, save, and give tell very little about your heart and its condition?

Hey, I'm only asking; I'll let God's Spirit do the rest. *I'm kidding!*

 [insert two-minute time span]

Feel anything? Just so you know, the Holy Spirit's nudging might feel like nervousness, conviction, or gas. So NOW do you feel anything?

OKAY, JUST CHECKING.

How You Spend

Yeah, so we talked a little about budgets in the last section. If you were paying attention, you probably remember that one of the main objectives for doing a budget is to know how and where your money is being spent. So here's the deal: If you didn't do the budget process in section 2 [you're a jerk face! (a name my wife calls me)], you should go and do that before continuing on [I can't believe you didn't do a budget] unless you already have a [I am not going to worry about this] working budget.

If you already have a budget—new or old—by all means, keep reading. For those of you who didn't do one, come over here. *Do it.* ⬇

Okay, listen. Perhaps I was too hard on you for not doing the budget. I know I can be a little over the top, but I'm only trying to help you. So be cool and just do the budget. It will help the rest of this book make sense. Would it hurt you that much to do it?

STOP ROLLING YOUR EYES.

No, you totally just rolled your eyes.

Okay, I give up.

Now look at your budget and separate your expenditures [places you owe or pay money to] into very detailed categories. I'm giving you some space below to write these down, but feel free to make your own spreadsheet if you don't like the idea of writing personal information in a book. However, resist lumping expenses into big categories; that won't help you. Okay, get separating.

Topic	Category	What you spend monthly
Church/ministry		
	Tithe	
	Parachurch	
	Child sponsor	
	Other charities	
What keeps you warm and dry		
	Mortgage/rent	
	Property taxes	
	Utilities	
	Fixing stuff	
What keeps you moving		
	Car payment	
	Car insurance	
	Gas	
	Car maintenance	
	Parking	
	Bus/subway	
	Registration	

Topic	Category	What you spend monthly
What keeps your tummy from growling		
	Grocery	
	Lunch expenses	
	Out to dinner	
	Pizza delivery	
	Starbucks	
What keeps you looking hot and fabulous		
	Haircut/color	
	Clothes	
	Nails	
	Shoes	
	Spa	
	Dry cleaning	
	Jewelry	
	Health club	
	Makeup	
	Toiletries	
	Other	
What keeps you awake at night		
	Visa/MasterCard	
	American Express	
	Discover	
	School loan	
	Bank loan	
	Other	
What keeps you sane		
	Satellite/cable	
	Phone/Internet	
	Cell phone	

Topic	Category	What you spend monthly
	Movies	
	Music	
	iTunes	
	Vacation	
	Other travel	
	Gifts	
	Concerts	
	Alcohol	
	Hobbies	
	Dogs/cats/fish	
	Other	
What keeps you feeling good and healthy		
	Doctor	
	Drugs	
	Dental/vision	
	Counseling	
	Physical therapy	
	Health insurance	
	Other	
What keeps you educated		
	School/college	
	Books	
	Supplies	
Miscellaneous		
	Life insurance	

►►**EXTRA:** If you really want to get technical, you should add up all of the categories within each topic to find out what percentage of your income is going to each topic.

Sometimes percentages can be a wake-up call, especially if you discover that 25 percent of your monthly income is being spent on keeping yourself looking good. *OUCH!*◄◄

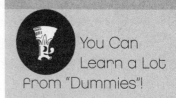

You Can Learn a Lot From "Dummies"!

In *Personal Finance for Dummies*, there's a three-point rule for "living within your means."

1 Spend less than you earn.

2 Save what you do not spend.

3 Invest what you save.[1]

Spendthrift

Let me cut to the chase here; the goal is to spend less than you make. I know it might *seem* like an easy concept, and some of you might have it mastered already. But for a lot of people — *myself included* — it's taking a bit longer to learn the art. Unfortunately, many of us twentysomethings and early thirtysomethings have grown accustomed to getting *what* we want *when* we want it. And it's made our spending habits look about as attractive as Rosie after *that* haircut. You saw the haircut, right?

Anyway, it's no secret that many of us either spend beyond our means or get as close to the mark as we can without saving a dime. This is a problem whether you make $20K, $120K, or $600K a year. Those of us who live like this tend to add things on to our lifestyle as our salary goes up. In other words, the more we make, the more we spend. Sure, not everyone is

Credit cards. You want to spend less? Get rid of the credit cards, especially if you have a problem keeping them in your wallet. Remember, those little plastic "friends" only make us *think* we have money.

Car loans. Too often we get in a hurry to have a new car, so we go out and sign a less-than-fabulous deal on a new car when we should be buying used or using our parents' hand-me-down. Think about what you could be doing with that three to six hundred dollars a month.

Stress. Yes, stress can cause you to overspend. It's easy to use our anxiety as an excuse to go shopping. Why? Because we claim it makes us feel better. Of course, you probably should know that shopping therapy only works temporarily!

Peer pressure. When you're around friends who seem to buy everything, it can be hard to say no. But most of the time these friends are only buying as a result of being around you — yep, it's a bad cycle.

No willpower. Seriously, some people have zero willpower when it comes to spending. They can't say no to sales, a to-die-for item of clothing, or anything that makes their TV echo throughout the house. *Come on*, people; learn to say *NO*!

Keeping up with the Joneses. If the neighbors have a new toy in their front lawn, you have to have one. When status is important, you can get into trouble and spend like crazy.

like this. Some of us are quite smart with money, but smart-money people—at least among young adults—are few and far between.

Now, most of us—even the smart ones—are probably able to look at how our money is being spent and see an apparent need to make some changes. Maybe it's in the way we save, the way we invest, or how generous we are with our money.

First, let's talk about some of the possible changes you might be able to make in regard to your saving. [Now, I realize that some of you aren't in debt or living beyond your means and therefore don't need to cut back for those reasons. If this is you, use these savings tips as a way to potentially give away more of your wealth to those who are in need.]

Saving
[where and how to cut your expenses down to size]

Two years ago, after being married for only three months, my wife and I changed the way we handle our money. Eighteen months before we were married I had lost my job and consequently had gotten into some pretty serious credit card debt. Though some of this debt was certainly a result of my selfish need to always have, have, have, a lot of it was based on simply attempting to survive.

We, the editors of *What You Didn't Learn from Your Parents About Money*, asked five people some questions about their buying habits — and then we guessed something about each of them.

In your opinion, your greatest purchase ever was	You wouldn't be caught dead buying anything at	Your last iTunes buy was	You're embarrassed to admit this, but you've spent money on
a drum set you never play [*Thank God.*]	a Christian bookstore [*Yeah, so now you think your first job at the Lighthouse Bookshop sucked.*]	Moby	porn
the sunroof on your Honda Civic	Old Navy	Chris Tomlin! [*You had to use an exclamation point, didn't you?*]	a thong
definitely the telescope you bought in tenth grade	Abercrombie & Fitch [*It's because of the ads, isn't it?*]	Skillet	You're not embarrassed about anything. [*Hint: tenth grade.*]
probably the cool jeans that you wear under a skirt	Sears	David Crowder Band!!!!!!	Michael Jackson's *Bad*
your Mac	Eh, you'll shop anywhere.	The Fray	a Duke University sweatshirt

The last thing you bought at a Christian bookstore was	The item you own that cost the most is	What we think your buying habits say about you:
Michael W. Smith's *I'll Lead You Home* — way back in 1995 [*Go West, young man.*]	your condo	Well, we think you're a twenty-six-year-old guy who *LOVES Relevant Magazine.*
the book *Do You Think I'm Beautiful?* [*Did you get an answer?*]	your car	No doubt you just graduated from Liberty University, but you're originally from Texas. Slightly overweight? *Okay, just checking.*
a card for your mom [*Aw!*]	a small fertilizer company [*Did not see that coming.*]	Well, we know you're single! And you were home-schooled. *Close?*
oh, the latest Joshua Harris book — you forget the name	your BMW	Wait, is this Rebecca St. James?
that *Purpose* book [*Wow.*]	your base-ball card collection	Well, you were once a col-lege jock, but an injury led you to become a Christian speaker. *Nailed you, didn't we?*

Survival is hardly what happened. When I said "I do" to my wife, I was, well, let's just say I was in a lot of debt. Credit card debt. [I will talk more about this in another section.]

Needless to say, I had pulled my wife into a very bad situation. However, instead of blaming me, getting angry, and resisting the urge to help, my wife, Jessica, joined forces with me, and together we began living life as two people on a mission to get out of debt and restore our financial stability.

Wow. It's a difficult journey. It's hard looking at your bride and not being able to give her everything in the world. It's been hard seeing her make sacrifices—not because of her own mistakes but because of mine. However, I do believe [and Jessica would admit to this, too] that God is using this struggle to teach us more about money.

But this required a change in our mind-set and in our money habits. **First things first: WE HAD TO CUT BACK!** We did a thorough study of our financial situation [basically, what I asked you to do earlier in this section] and found many ways in which we were crippling our ability to live a healthy and godly financial lifestyle.

In the area of saving money, our situation was ridiculous. Not only were we in debt up to our necks, but we were also spending every dollar we had on a lot of stuff we didn't need. One evening, after a pretty heated discussion about money, we prayed with each other and then began looking for ways both of us could change — not only to be smarter with our money but also to stop being stupid with our money.

I will be telling a lot of our personal financial story throughout the rest of this book, but in this section, I want to share with you a few points that will help you cut your spending. Of course, I probably don't need to tell you that Jessica and I haven't been perfect in our quest to become debt free; it's hard! We've wasted money along the way. However, when we do make a stupid decision, we're pretty quick to get back on track and begin again the journey toward thinking about money the way we believe God would have us think about it.

>> **ALERT!!** I know this will seem nearly impossible, but here's your goal: Invest 10 to 20 percent of your income toward either losing your debt or increasing your savings. You're probably thinking, *Matthew, that is crazy!*<<

You're probably right, and with that attitude it is impossible. And just cutting back will probably not give you 10 to 20 percent. It will more than likely take more sacrifice than you think. But I'll get to that soon enough!

Here are some ideas to help you look for ways to save money. [Now, please know that not all of these ideas will apply to your situation, but they should at least give you a good place to start your own journey.]

Two Things Before You Begin!

1 **Pray.** This might seem simple, but if you're a follower of Jesus, you know that prayer works. But don't expect God to suddenly perform a financial miracle in your life [he may, but don't expect that]; sometimes it's the *process* that God wants us to experience. He's not always about saving the day. However, when you pray you might ask him to help you embrace the mind-set of stewardship.

2 **Get desperate.** Don't laugh; sometimes desperation is exactly what we need to begin this process of changing our habits. If you don't feel the urgency to make changes, then you probably won't. God cares very much how you handle the money he has bestowed to you. He wants you to save, to be out of debt, and to be able to live generously. I once heard financial expert Dave Ramsey tell an audience, "If you're not feeling absolutely desperate, you're not ready to pursue living the financial lifestyle God has for you." Umm, *and he's an expert.* So either get desperate or ask God to give you the tenacity it takes to make these changes!

Ideas for Reducing the Money You Spend!

[in no particular order, rhyme, or reason — well, on second thought, a couple of them might rhyme]

Very Easy Ways to Save on Electricity

You don't want to spend too much time thinking about ways to save money via electricity, but here are three ideas you might consider. Of course, the bigger your home, the more money you can save following these suggestions.

 Raise/lower your thermometer. By setting your thermometer two to three degrees warmer in the summer and lowering your thermometer by two to three degrees in the winter, you can save somewhere between $15 and $30 a month. You might not think this is much, but when you're shelling out $90 instead of $120 at the end of the month, you'll probably be happy enough to do a little dance.

 Turn the heating element off on your dishwasher. Let the dishes air dry. Sure, your glasses might show a few extra spots, but who cares? You can wipe them off when company comes over. And if you're feeling really thrifty, wash your dishes by hand!

 Wash all clothes in cold water. Eh, you might think this is a dumb idea, and perhaps it is a bit over the top, but your hot-water heater uses a lot of energy. [**EXTRA:** Your water heater doesn't need to be set any higher than 120 degrees.]

How About This for *BIG* Savings on Electricity? Resist TV!

According to Michael Bluejay, it's estimated that if you were to stop watching TV, you would save $82 a year in electricity bills.[2] *Yeah, that's not worth it!*

Harsh Reality! A Few Things You Don't Need

[if you need to get drastic — and some of you do — here are eight things you don't really need to be spending money on — at least for right now]

 You don't need cable or satellite TV. This is a quick way to save $50 to $90 a month, depending on your service. Now, if you have cable for reception purposes, do basic cable. Yes, I know this is a bit out of your comfort zone, but trust me: You don't *really* need it. And when you're back on your feet again, you can choose whether or not it's an expense you want to incur. [*And, truly, you can live without TBS, ESPN, and HBO!*]

 You don't need Starbucks. Yep, a life without Starbucks is a cruel existence for many of us. But those of us who frequent "the Bucks" three to four times a week [some of us a lot more] are shelling out $50 a month on coffee! Why not buy the beans and make the coffee at home? [*I told you this wouldn't be easy!*]

 You don't need a cell phone *and* a landline [if you live in an area with good reception]. My advice? Consider dropping the landline. You want to have a second cell battery on hand for emergencies, but by losing the landline, you can save $30 to $50 a month.

You don't need alcohol. Even if you're simply the casual drinker, "adult refreshments" are pricey, and if you're buying the cheap stuff, you're probably not drinking for mere refreshment.

Nine Ways to Save When Shopping

❶ Buy generic when it's practical.
❷ Clip coupons.
❸ Watch for bright yellow smiley faces bouncing through Wal-Mart.
❹ Buy in bulk when practical.
❺ Buy holiday supplies *after* the holiday [for the following year].
❻ Shop for stuff you need, not for fun.
❼ Stop buying bottled water.
❽ Make a shopping list.
❾ Plan your gift giving ahead of time and buy things on clearance.

You don't need to eat out more than once a week. Perhaps the biggest waste of money is attending those after-church gatherings at TGI Friday's or Ruby Tuesday. Jessica and I realized we were spending between $200 and $300 a month on eating out—*and we didn't go to expensive restaurants*! So eating out is not only *unhealthy*, but it's also expensive! Hey, check your receipts; you'd probably be surprised at how much you're spending.

You don't need to pick up the tab. The next time a friend says, "I'm sorry; I can't afford to eat out today," your response does not need to be, "Oh, don't worry about it; I got you." I have no idea how much money I squandered by paying for other people's meals. It's a bad habit! So stop it.

You don't need a pet. *Sorry,* I know that seems harsh, but Fido and Fluffy are costing you a fortune. A friend of mine recently spent $1,200 to get a dog's broken leg fixed—*$1,200!* But, hey, even a healthy pet, when you consider the cost of food, vet bills, and toys, is a pricey expenditure. And, honestly, your friends don't have the heart to tell you this, but *your house stinks!* Lose the pet.

You don't need a $90 haircut *or* your nails done every ten days. Yes, some people [mostly women] do spend *$90* or more on a haircut. And believe me, I know [because of my wife] the value of a good cut, but come on, you can probably find a good cut for half that amount—*at least!* And while you're at it, do your nails yourself.

How to Save Money on Car Insurance

I hate shopping for things like car insurance. It's stressful for me. I don't like calling strangers, I don't like filling out surveys online, and I'm not a fan of the large amounts of junk mail I get when I begin hunting down a new option for things like insurance, loans, and investments. However, insurance is a pretty important commodity. At least that's what we've been taught to think. In some states, having insurance is the law, and because of the costs involved if you have a car accident—hospital fees and car repairs being the biggest threats—that's probably a good thing. But you don't need to overpay for your car insurance. Here are a few ideas to help you avoid overspending!

Keep that driving record clean! This seems obvious, I know. But you'd be surprised at how many people still don't realize that the amount they spend on insurance goes up—*way up*—when their driving record is less than perfect. [*I shouldn't be surprised, really; some people also eat Spam.*] Of course, tickets happen. [*Some of you know quite well that they happen!*] When they do happen, make sure you go through all of the proper legal channels to do everything possible to get those *bad* points off your record. Some states will let you take a driving course to *work* points off your record. Some states make you go through a waiting period. Contact your local DMV to find out what's available in your town.

Shop, shop, shop! When Jessica and I began shopping for new car insurance, we were paying $179 a month. After calling what seemed like countless insurance companies, we finally found the *same* coverage [*at a more respectable company*] for $149 a month. So it definitely pays to shop!

Avoid buying cars known for speed! You can live without the ability to travel at 140 mph; the faster your car can go, the higher your insurance will be—it's as easy as that. Also, avoid *black* and *red* cars—insurance for these rides are a bit more expensive.

Know your discounts! Every safety feature your car possesses—anti-lock brakes, anti-theft devices, and airbags—is a reduction in your premium!

Pay your six-month premium in whole! For Jessica and me, this wasn't an option, but if we had been able to, we would have saved about $14 a month. Many insurance companies charge a fee when you pay the premium in installments.

 Drive a junker! Insurance for *new* or *newer* cars is more expensive, mainly because *collision insurance* is a must! But do you really need to be riding around in a new car? Probably not! [Unless you do a ton of traveling.] To avoid paying those high prices on insurance, consider driving a piece of crap for a while. Believe me, if your girl *really* loves you, she won't leave you for a man with a Hummer. And if she does, *accidentally* crash into the dude's Hummer—remember, you've got a *junker* and don't care! [Yes, I was kidding—mostly!]

 Check out Progressive.com! Yeah, you've seen the commercials; Progressive will give you not only their rates but also the rates of three or four of their competition. Sounds too good to be true, but sometimes good things happen.

Other, Less Practical Ways to Save on Car Insurance!

→ **Become an engineer!** Drivers with degrees in engineering are apparently *safer* than drivers with other degrees.

→ **Become a teacher!** Many insurance companies give teachers a break — *just because they're teachers.*

→ **Join the military!** Some insurance companies [like Geico, for instance] give extra discounts to active military.

→ **Be old!** Yep, that's right; if you can prove you're of AARP age, you can get a discount.[3]

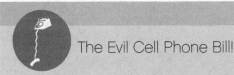

The Evil Cell Phone Bill!

I'm sure we have all, at one time or another, encountered a big surprise when opening the cell phone bill. "Dude," one of my friends once said, "my cell phone bill was $200! I couldn't believe it." Yeah, the cell phone is a great invention, but the cell phone bill can be a *terrorist attack* on a budget if you're not careful. Here's what you need to look out for.

Stop sending text messages and pictures via your phone! Unless you have a deal that includes it, most cell phone companies are making you pay extra for any text messages over one hundred per month! And some services make you pay for every picture you send. So know the limitations of your program and stick to them.

Know the dates of your program! Most of us probably don't know what day of the month our minutes start over. In fact, we might assume it's the first of the month. But such is not the case. Call costumer service and find out what date your service switches to a NEW month. Then check how you're doing with minutes a couple of times a month to avoid charges for going over.

Remember, when you change time zones, so does your cell phone service! I've been screwed on this more than a few times. I assumed that when I was in California [Pacific Time], my phone still worked on Central Time. *NO!* Yeah, so when 9 p.m. Central Time came around [while I was basking in California at 7:00 p.m. Pacific Time], I thought my minutes were free. Boy, did I get a surprise.

Stop downloading games and new ringtones! I know it's tempting to have the latest ringtones and games downloaded to your phone, but you're wasting a lot of money. And, not to mention, your Missy Elliott ringtone is annoying the rest of us.

Okay, so not all of us can afford the wardrobe of Paris Hilton or Prince Harry. Sadly, many of us, when desiring to dress like an heir or heiress, whip out our plastic and buy, buy, buy. In the end, we look great, but we fall into debt, and let's face it: That's *very* un-Hilton-like. But I've got good news: You don't have to pull out the plastic and spend a fortune to put on your best fashion statement. You just have to shop smart and be willing to work at it!

Here are my top eight tips for buying fashion you can afford!

※ **If you don't love it, don't buy it.** It doesn't matter if it's a good deal; if you don't love how those jeans accentuate all that your mama gave you, then don't buy them. Poor-fitting jeans that are $10 [down from $60] are a waste of your money — and you know it!

※ **Watch your back, baby.** Clearance is never in the front of the store, so don't start your shopping there. Remember, full price on *anything* is a complete rip-off. Don't buy it unless it's at least 50 percent off! Every major specialty and department store puts last season's fashions on clearance, and if you're willing to dress one season behind, your wallet will thank you.

※ **Learn your favorite store's bargain patterns.** It may take some time for you to master the art, but all stores have patterns in how they mark items down. For instance, when Target clearance is as low as it is going to go, the price usually ends in a four. The Gap usually drops prices 25 to 30 percent before slashing them to 40 to 50 percent a month later. You might try visiting some shopping forums online to learn what more experienced shoppers already know about your favorite store and to hear how they do sales/clearance. A couple websites to check out are www.fatwallet.com and www.slickdeals.net. **HINT:** Many stores do their markdowns the third week of the month!

※ **Pay attention to the little things.** Sometimes clothing that is marked "clearance" doesn't sell because it has a small flaw, such as a loose button or an open seam. Most of the time if you point the flaw out, the store will give you an additional discount on the item.

- ✄ **Shop often.** When you routinely visit your favorite stores, you will be able to keep a close eye on when the items you want are on sale or clearance. If you don't regularly shop at the store where you want a particular item, you will be more apt to buy it at full price.

- ✄ **Check online.** Many stores offer better deals online. Or you might look for the item you want to purchase at eBay.com or Overstock.com! [But be careful of wholesale sellers on eBay — they're probably selling the clothes illegally.]

- ✄ **Sign up for e-mail newsletters.** E-mail newsletters are a great way to learn about sales and discounts. Sometimes e-lerts will include coupons, special discounts, or frequent-shopper offers.

- ✄ **Clue others in.** When you hear about a good deal, don't keep it to yourself; tell your friends! If you do, they'll be more apt to let you in on a good deal when they find one.

BONUS TIPS!

- ✄ Shop at Marshalls, T.J.Maxx, and outlet stores! These stores carry brand-name fashion at discounted prices. [Plan to take your time; these stores can be a bit overwhelming.]

- ✄ All of us have a favorite high-end store where even the clearance is out of our price range. But if you pop in at the end of each buying season — August for summer, March for winter — you might discover a deal you can't refuse. [I once bought a $400 suit for $38!]

- ✄ Retro-clothing stores are a great place to find creative and cheap accessories. And a good accessory — such as a scarf, brooch, or hat — can make an ordinary outfit stellar.

- ✄ Whenever you travel, make sure you set aside some cash for shopping. Your favorite stores often offer local deals or styles that are not available in your town!

- ✄ Buy the Sunday paper! You need to be in the know about sales! How can you be a smart shopper if you don't know where to find the deals?

➠ For great ideas and tips, visit TheBudgetFashionista.com [Be Fabulous for Less]! Not only will you find out about good deals, but you'll also enjoy laughing at this woman's musings about shopping online.

Though ordering takeout might be easier [and fortune cookies are fun in bed], buying groceries and eating at home will save you money. You will save even more ch-ching by following a few simple rules.

1. Take advantage of store sales. First, grab a sales ad [probably in your local newspaper] and VIC [Very Important Customer] card [these cards make sales automatic for frequent customers]. Every week, certain food items go on sale. Some stores, such as Publix, will give everyone the sale price, while other stores will give the sale price only to those who have the store's VIC card. Do not be a casual card user. Instead, buy items when they are on sale. For instance, Matthew and I love pork tenderloin, but at $16 a cut, it doesn't quite fit in our weekly grocery budget. However, about once every four to six weeks, our local grocery store has a buy one, get one free special. Usually I will jump on that, sometimes even buying two and therefore getting two free! Wa-hoo! *Nothing like saving $32 on pig.*

2. Clip coupons. While you may feel like your grandma at first, clipping coupons will eventually make you feel great! You can find coupons a few ways; the easiest is by subscribing to your city's Sunday paper. Don't worry; it will amaze you how quickly your newspaper subscription will pay for itself — and how much money you'll save because of it. You can also get coupons online [just Google *coupons*] or by calling your favorite brands' 1-800 numbers, telling customer service how much you like their products, and requesting coupons.

There are a couple of ways to maximize your coupon usage:

- Combine coupons with grocery-store savings. So when cereal is on sale for $1.98, use the coupon you have for $.50 off.
- Use your coupons at grocery stores that double coupons [yes, some stores do this]. Some grocery stores will double coupons up to $.50 or even $.99. As you can imagine, your savings can skyrocket, particularly if you have a great coupon for a sale item.

NOTE: Some stores that offer buy one, get one free will ring each item at half price, allowing you to use *two* coupons instead of just one! Paying attention to these little details can make a huge difference on your grocery bill. Also, if you clip coupons already, you've probably noticed that $.99 coupons are rare. This is because of the doubling offers given by grocery stores; by changing the savings to $1, the manufacturers avoid having to pay the "up to a dollar" doubling rate.

Expiration dates are the trickiest part of coupons. Manufacturers put dates on coupons so people will use them right away. But chances are you'll be like me, and you'll still have the coupon after it has expired. That's okay. Most clerks don't notice and will accept the coupon anyway. I find it is particularly effective to go to a male cashier. For some reason, guys don't seem to pay much attention to expiration dates.

I have made it a game each week to see how much I can save between coupons and store savings. Some weeks I do a lot better than others, but on average I save $60 to $80 a month. So if you have the patience, it is totally worth it.

3. Make a list. When shopping, you will save money if you stick to what is on your list. The only time you should deviate is if the store is offering a special sale and you can get a great deal. It helps to keep a magnetic notepad on the fridge so you can keep track during the week of things you are running low on. That way, you won't forget what you need when you are making your big list once a week.

4. Plan your menu weekly. Planning your meals for the week will eliminate your need to make extra trips to the grocery store. When you go to the grocery store for an item you need for dinner, you often come out with several bags! These multiple trips to the grocery store add up to extra dollars you wouldn't have spent if you had done all of your shopping at once. I tend to do all my shopping for the week on Sunday because it's easiest for me and I'm able to use the coupons from that day's paper, but do what works best for you.

5. Look for expiration dates. You can save significantly on items that are close to expiring [like meat and bread] if you buy them on the day they are marked down. Learn the system, or at least learn to keep an eye out for the stickers on these markdowns. If you buy these items, be sure to eat them that day or put them in the freezer to eat at a later date.

6. Look for the marked-down-items aisle. Your grocery store may also have a special spot where it puts discounted or discontinued items. Check there on your weekly trips to the store because you can find incredible bargains.

7. Buy produce. Eating in-season fresh fruits and vegetables is less expensive than eating processed items. You can save even more money on produce by buying it directly from a farmer's market or food stand. Even if this isn't possible, you will still save at the grocery store, just not as much because of the middleman involvement.

8. Shop high and low. It is common knowledge that the most expensive items tend to be chest level in the grocery store. Therefore, when grocery shopping, be sure to look a little higher and a little lower to make sure you are really getting what you need and not just what you know the best.

9. Shop full. Don't shop on an empty stomach because it's a well-known reality that we all tend to buy more sweets and carbs — and just more in general — when we're hungry.

Have you ever gone shopping on black Friday? Do you even know what black Friday is? Black Friday, the day after Thanksgiving, is the busiest shopping day of the year and the kickoff to the Christmas shopping season. Well, I want to challenge you to start your Christmas shopping on December 26. That's right — an entire year before Christmas. I feel a list coming on. . . .

1 Start early. No joke, every year since I was about twelve I have started my Christmas shopping for the next year the day after Christmas. It has always been a tradition that my family would get up at about 5:45 a.m., get to Target by 6:30, and rush in when the doors opened at 7:00, along with fifty to one hundred other mad women [and a few men]. You see, everything is marked 50 percent off, including all Christmas gift items [like those great car packages for Dad], so you can get a ton of great stuff. So thanks to the Christmas money from Grandma, my wallet was set to do a little shopping and get a lot of bang for my buck! By starting early [even if December 26 is a little extreme] and spreading your spending throughout the year, your checking account will not take such a hit in November and December. Moreover, you will be less tempted to charge gifts [as many people do]. Most important, you can buy things on sale and clearance!

2 Sales. I hit on this in number one, but just to reiterate, shop for items on sale. It does not mean you think less of your friend or family member if you buy something on sale or clearance; it just means you are being a smart shopper.

3 Free shipping. As Internet shopping becomes increasingly popular [online Christmas gift buying was up 24 percent in 2005 according to CBS[4]], chances are you will buy at least one gift online. Most e-tailers offer free shipping throughout the year and especially around the holidays. Check your favorite sites often to watch for these bargains and sign up for companies' e-mail newsletters as well. In addition to potentially scoring info about free shipping, you will also stay updated about the latest fads and happenings at your favorite e-tailers.

4 **Handmade gifts.** This obviously won't work for everyone, but for some people, handmade gifts are the best [both to give and to receive]. And making gifts is often more cost effective than buying them. While in college, I wanted to give gifts to a bunch of my girlfriends, but I had a limited budget, so I decided to make each of them scarves. They turned out great, and my friends loved the personal and thoughtful gift. The sky is the limit when it comes to creative gifts — scrapbooks, jewelry, knitting, painting. As my mom always said, it's the thought that counts.

5 **Don't go overboard.** This may sound a bit foolish, but many people have a tendency to go overboard when it comes to gift giving at Christmas. They want their gifts to be the best, and they don't want people to think they didn't spend enough. Thinking like this is not healthy, nor is it necessary. Christmas is not about how much a gift costs nor how many gifts you give, so do not get caught up in that. If you do, you will end up spending more money than necessary! Christmas is NOT an excuse to give, give, and give some more. If you have the finances to do it, that's fine! But if you're spending your last dollar on buying Aunt Gerty another vase, SAVE YOUR MONEY!

Save Money or Begin Chipping Away at Your Debt!

[whatever you do, don't just let it sit in your checking account]

Like I said earlier, the goal is to put 10 to 20 percent in your savings account or toward outstanding debt. You can cut as much as you want out of your budget, but if you don't make a proactive effort to get that money out of your checking account and into a savings account, retirement fund, or money market account, you're not helping your cause. Here are some pointers on saving!

Reward Yourself!

Don't become so rigid in your thinking that you fail to have fun. Remember, stewardship is about handling the money God has given you with wisdom, but it's not about *never* thinking about yourself. It's true that God wants us to enjoy our lives, too. In order to not get burned out by this journey, you have to reward yourself once in a while with a little splurge. What I mean is this: You have to budget some *fun* into your financial plan. If you've done really well in cutting back and you're finally at a place where you're spending less than what you make, reward yourself! You could reward yourself with a trip to the spa, an iPod, a mini-vacation, or a new outfit. Don't go into debt showing yourself some love; that would be stupid! However, once in a while, plan on thinking about *me* [you, not me].

※ **Make a plan/set a goal.** Mentally set a goal of how much money you want to save and begin strategizing on how you're going to get there.

※ **Start small and build.** Don't set an insurmountable goal. Begin small [like 5 to 8 percent] and build on that.

※ **Do whatever is necessary to ensure you don't spend your savings.** Once you've gotten some cash saved up, you're probably going to be tempted to spend it. Here are some suggestions!

- ▣ Put a percentage away in a retirement fund that you don't have access to.

- ▣ Send it to your mom and dad to put in their bank; just tell Dad you're too weak to handle that kind of money.

- ▣ Open a five to ten year Certificate of Deposit. [CDs are safe, and big fees are incurred for early withdrawal.]

- **Arrange with your employer for a portion of your earnings to go directly into your savings and/or retirement account [I'll talk about your options in the next section].** Most employers allow your check to be directly deposited into more than one account. One thing to know is this: If you are putting money into a retirement account, this money is pretaxed. In other words [or numbers], let's say that before taxes you make $1,200 every two weeks; after taxes, you make $879 [that's a 26.75 percent deduction from your paycheck for Uncle Sam]. *Okay, you still with me?* Let's pretend you're having a hard time deciding whether you want to put $100 into your retirement fund or $100 into your savings. [*And remember, you could do both, or you could split the $100 between the two—but I don't want to confuse you!*] If you chose to go the retirement fund route, you would take more money home with you! Maybe you're thinking, *How is that possible?* It's called *pretaxed*, baby! Let me show you the difference:
  - **Retirement fund.** In a retirement fund, your $100 comes out of your paycheck *before* Uncle Sam gets his cut. So your $1,200 minus $100 would equal $1,100 *before* taxes. Let's subtract the 26.75 percent! Your paycheck would NOW be $805.75.
  - **Savings.** Because you're simply putting your money into a savings account [one that you could spend if you wanted], your $100 would come out *after* taxes. Since

your take-home amount was $879, if you were to put $100 in savings, the new amount to be deposited into your checking account would be $779.

The difference is $26.75. [*Pretty cool, huh!*] Of course, Uncle Sam will get his cut when you withdraw that retirement fund thirty or forty years from now.

Like I mentioned before, you could put $50 into one and $50 into another OR put $100 into both. Remember, you should talk to your employer [more than likely, the human resources department] to find out your tax rate and also what your take-home amount would be. *You still have to pay your bills.*

🎌 **Put your "savings" toward debt.** If you have debt [*again, we'll talk about this in the next section — yippee!*], you should build your savings up to a certain amount [$1,000 is a nice round number] and then begin kicking your debt's @$$ like it just insulted your mother. Umm, did that make sense?

The Stuff
Grown-Ups Do

If you're gonna screw
up, do it while you're
young. The older you
get, the harder it is to
bounce back.

— Winston Groom

When I was twenty-five years old, I made my first big purchase: a new car—an Oldsmobile Alero, to be exact. However, at the time, the where/when/how of buying a car was all new territory for me. In other words, I knew I was going to have spend money, but I didn't really know what to look for or how to negotiate.

As a kid, I had witnessed my dad purchase a new car. As long as I remained quiet while he negotiated, he'd let me sit right next to him while he "dickered" [a term he used] with the car salesperson. My dad sometimes scared me when he dickered.

[Here's a story about one of my father's car purchases I remember well.]

Though they were a bit unsure about the color white, Mom and Dad decided to put an offer down on a brand-new Chevy Celebrity. Dad knew his offer was low. Heck, I didn't know anything about cars, but even I knew the offer was low.

"Teddy," said my dad seriously, "my wife and I talked, and we're willing to pay $9,000 for that white Chevy Celebrity."

Dad had a couple of things going for him. His credit history was stellar. And when it came to parting ways with his hard-earned money, Dad was stubborn.

Teddy, the young, somewhat inexperienced car salesman, began crunching numbers. After a couple of minutes had gone by, he looked up at my dad.

"Now, Mr. Turner, that's a good car out there. I believe the best I can do is $10,105," said Teddy.

As soon as the counter offer came out of Teddy's mouth, my heart began to race. I knew Dad was not going to like it.

"Is that the best you can do, Teddy?" said my dad in his very disappointed and "don't mistake me for an idiot" tone of voice. Dad took off his hat, ran his hand through his hair, and put his hat back on, something he does when he gets nervous.

"Well, Mr. Turner, I think it is," said Teddy, looking down at his calculator. After a couple of minutes went by, Teddy looked up. "WAIT! I think I've worked up an offer you won't be able to refuse."

"Okay, let's hear it."

My nerves began to make noises in my stomach. My eyes wandered back and forth between the moderately heated scene going on here in Teddy's office and my sister and mother, who were outside in the car, waiting to hear whether or not Dad would be buying a car.

"$9,800. How does that sound?"

"Teddy, I don't think you're hearing me; I'm only paying $9,000 for that car," said Dad in a stern, definitive voice. "If you can meet that offer, fine. If not, just tell me."

"Mr. Turner, there is no way I can let that car leave this lot for $9,000!" said Teddy, who was obviously becoming frustrated by my father's unwillingness to make one move on his offer. "Would you do $9,400?"

"Nope."

"Oh, come on, Mr. Turner; you're not working with me here."

"Teddy, I've already told you what my offer is. If you can't meet it, then I'm getting in my car and I'm driving up the road to the next Chevy dealership and buying my car there. Do you want my money or not?"

Well, to make a long story a little bit shorter, my dad eventually got the price he wanted—*$9,000!* My sister and I were *SO* excited—mainly because this was the first car Mom and Dad had bought that included a cassette player already built in. [*And, yes, it was one of the newer kinds that featured the ability to turn the tape over without taking it out of the player—ah, technology.*]

When I was thirteen, I couldn't have imagined having to negotiate with a car salesperson like I had just witnessed my father do. Dad was consistent and firm, and in my personal opinion, he was also a little bit gruff.

At thirteen I hated being gruff toward an individual. Not that I couldn't be gruff; it just wasn't one of my favorite things. Back then, partly because of this experience, I feared the financial handlings of grown-ups. They seemed forced and uncomfortable. Unfortunately, when I bought my first new car at age twenty-five, gruff still didn't come all that naturally to me. Honestly, being consistent and firm didn't come all that naturally to me either.

So when I bought that first car, my father came along. He went with me to all the dealerships. He did all the dickering. Asked all the questions. And he got me the price I wanted.

What You Didn't Learn from Your Parents About Money Presents:

A Will and a Way — Answers to Your Most Intriguing Questions About Having a Will!

QUESTION: What is a will?

ANSWER: Oh, we think whoever asked this question is a bona fide genius. *We're so lying!* Like, if you don't know what a will is by the time you're twenty, consider yourself *a few fries short of a Happy Meal*! We're kidding. You're smart; you know it! You're smart; you show it! [Say it two more times.] Sure, it's a simple question, but we totally think it's still a good one. Honey, a will is just a legal document that declares how you want your property dispersed when you die. *Spooky!* You might think it's a little weird talking about a will [*it's eerie having to think about death — like we said, spooky!*]. And though you probably don't need a will, well, unless you own anything of real value [and you don't] or importance [nope, none of that either] or you're married [sex is great, BTW!], it's important to know *about* the making of a will. Writing a will is one of

Oh, the trials of having to grow up and do grown-up things.

I hate growing up, Papa Smurf!

— *Grumpy Smurf*

Grumpy Smurf might have been on to something. We all have experienced the difficulties of growing up. Of course, the physical parts of growing up aren't difficult; they just happen — *usually*. But even though our bodies naturally go through all the necessary changes that accompany maturity, embracing many of the *responsibilities* that come with growing up tends to come less naturally.

For a lot of us "late bloomers," financial responsibility — or the lack of — is often one of the most challenging areas of all the grown-up things we experience. Let's face it: Some of the more important financial mechanics scare us mainly because we don't know what the heck we're doing. When it comes to things like buying a car, buying a house, investing, getting out of debt, or planning for retirement, many of us are pretty much clueless.

Well, this part of the book is going to change some of that. Of course, after reading this section, you won't suddenly be an expert, but you will be informed. And for a lot of these things, being informed is a good place to start.

those grown-up things you should learn about. [Matthew wrote that last sentence; you can tell because it's *boring*!]

QUESTION: What does a will do?

ANSWER: Okay, so were you reading that last answer? Like we said before, a will ensures that all of your property gets distributed to the individuals and/or organizations that you desire. We know you'd rather see your daddy's estranged cousin be boiled in tar than see him get his hands on your Gucci shoes. Are we right? *Well, maybe that's just us; we don't want our cousin Sue getting anything.* It also protects your wealth from going to places, causes, and people you don't want it to, *like any charity involving Barbra Streisand*. Sorry, we're so NOT fans!

QUESTION: Do I need a will?

ANSWER: Do you *know* how to read? We've explained this already. You should be *thinking* about it now [you know, because you're reading something about it]. But you don't have to write a will until you're married; you need a will when you're married just in case something were to happen to you or your spouse. It's good to know your spouse's wishes! Or if you're single and you own real estate or any property of value, you should have a will. *We're still pretty confident you don't have to worry about that.*

QUESTION: How do I go about making a will?

ANSWER: Oh, this is actually quite simple. ① You have to figure out what properties you want to distribute. ② Begin making decisions on who will inherit your property. In other words:

⇨ Kenny, my brother, gets my beard trimmer.
⇨ My cousin James gets my bedspread.
⇨ Aunt Nel gets my *Dogs Playing Poker* framed picture.
⇨ My ex-girlfriend Jenny gets all of my Michael W. Smith CDs.

See what we mean? This stuff is simple, right? You can actually have a little fun when writing a will. Heck, you can even leave those "you've been left behind" weird messages. ③ Pick an executor [we think you should get a hot one!] of your will. Basically,

Almost Everything You Need to Know About Buying a Hot Car

[or a junker, minivan, SUV, Mini Cooper, or Toyota]

Car commercials tend to be dorky. In fact, only commercials for mattresses, funeral homes, and that old Summer's Eve commercial [the one with a mother and daughter walking down a beach, talking about "freshness"] come close to being as cheesy and awkward as car dealerships' commercials.

 Insert cheesy jingle:

We've got hundreds of cars, trucks, but not tanks
No money down and that's no prank
If you buy today, we offer our thanks
With five hundred cash back today at Frank's!

[fat guy named Frank stands next to a black car]

FRANK: Are you looking for a new car or truck? You've gotta come to Frank's! At Frank's Cars and Trucks you're treated like family. . . .

You've seen car commercials similar to this one, right? I'm not so sure this kind of ad strategy really helps car salespeople's reputations. I mean, a lot of people already hold a bit of distrust toward salespeople. I don't think commercials featuring a man dressed in a power suit yelling into the camera about how good his cars are help the car-salesperson image all that much.

But those commercials must be pretty effective, considering that people are still buying cars. Or maybe it's just that almost all of us need cars.

an executor ensures that the demands of the will get carried out. [In other words, he or she would make sure Aunt Nel got her picture!] ④ Umm, if you have any kiddies, choose a guardian for them. [Yeah, this is where it gets a bit strange — choosing a person to watch your kids can be a precarious decision. Just don't make it too emotional.] ⑤ After you write your will [Do-it-yourself legal website Nolo.com recommends using Quicken WillMaker for all of your will needs!], sign it in front of a witness: a notary public or lawyer. [*And BAM!, your will is written!*][1]

Tootles!

>>The editors

PS: If you still need help, e-mail us at WeLoveWritingFor Matthew@yahoo.com.

Five Reasons You Shouldn't Buy a Car

5 If you're in debt up to your eyeballs [or even your kneecaps], you shouldn't buy a car.

4 If you're unable to put 15 to 20 percent of the cost down, you shouldn't buy a car.

3 If you're blind, you shouldn't buy a car.

2 If you're incapable of paying your current bills, you shouldn't buy a car.

1 If you're jobless, you shouldn't buy a car.

However, let's face it: Buying a car can be an overwhelming task. Just Google "car-buying tips" and you'll discover hundreds of websites that offer their best help. It seems like everyone with any kind of platform has advice to offer and warnings to heed when it comes to car buying. Sifting through all the information on what to do when you're about to buy a car is daunting, and that's before you even step foot into a dealership's showroom.

So what should you do? Umm, well, have you thought about riding your bike to work? Maybe a horse? A scooter? A really large relative? Yeah, I know this isn't helping you.

[Okay, moving on.]

Like everything in this book, my advice is far from exhaustive. But my direction will certainly help you feel more prepared when buying a car. And if my words don't help, *call my father.*

He'll definitely get you the best deal. Let's get started!

First rule: Do the research!

When you're in the market to buy a new or used car, research will be one of the most important components of your car-buying experience.

Depending on your situation, taking the time to research not only the car but also who you're buying it from can some-times save you hundreds or even thousands of dollars. Research will also equip you with the knowledge of what you want and don't want, as well as what questions you should ask the sales-person about the cars you are interested in. Finally, research will help you determine how much money you should expect to pay—and what price would be a great deal. These days, research is simpler than it was several years ago. Today websites do the research for you—or at least a large chunk of it. Don't reinvent the wheel—start out with the following list and go to the car manufacturers' websites, and you will have a good start.

Cars.com. At Cars.com, you can buy new and used cars, do research, and even get shopping advice. This site has everything related to cars [even movie trailers of films coming out about cars], and it should definitely be part of your car-shopping plan.

Researching Cars? You Might Also Try These Sites

- ▶ Vehix.com
- ▶ Autobytel.com
- ▶ Edmunds.com
- ▶ BuyingAdvice.com
- ▶ CarSmart.com

▦ ConsumerReports.com. You've no doubt heard about Consumer Reports. What once was a large, thick book that Dad would go to the library to find is now an easy-to-use website. Everything you could possibly need to know about a car's good points, bad points, and cost is featured here.

Other Ideas for Research

Go to the library. Most public libraries have the latest books detailing all the car information you should need to make a good decision.

Ask other car owners. If you know of someone who has an older model of the car you want to purchase, don't be afraid to contact him or her to see if he or she might be able to answer some of the questions you have regarding the make, model, and efficiency of your desired car.

Talk to your favorite mechanic. Since mechanics work on cars all day long, they tend to have the inside scoop on the good, bad, and ugly of cars. So you might want to get your mechanic's opinion before you buy.

A Couple of Things to Know About Incentives and Rebates

What's the Kelley Blue Book?

The Kelley Blue Book is an independent company that determines valuations of cars. Its website is www.kbb.com, and according to Kelley Blue Book, nearly one in three Americans who have bought or sold a vehicle have visited the site since it was started in 1995.

Remember in 2005 when it seemed like every car manufacturer was offering employee discounts to try to lure people to buy their cars? At the time, it was a bit hard to discern who was offering the best deal, mainly because it seemed like everyone was offering the *same* deal. Generally speaking, incentives and rebates are a bit hard to follow. Here are a few things to know.

First, *rebates* are offered by the manufacturer directly to you. The dealership [or where you buy your car] is not financially affected by a rebate. It might help if you were to think of a rebate like you would the coupon for Duncan Hines brownies that you cut out from the Sunday paper. The grocery store where you use the coupon is not taking the $.99 hit; Duncan Hines is giving you the break. In the same way, the dealership isn't losing any money when a rebate is offered, so don't let the salesperson play the "I can't go any lower" game. More than likely, he or she can. Oftentimes car buyers resist negotiating for the best price because of the rebate and consequently end up paying more for the vehicle than necessary.

Now, *incentives* are usually special deals that the manufacturer offers dealerships, and if the dealer chooses, the savings are handed down to you. However, be cautious of incentives. Many times incentives are used to lower the discounts that would otherwise have been given to you. According to the experts, there are no free lunches when it comes to purchasing cars! More than likely, the deal has been worked into the price, and you're not saving as much as you might think.

Always read the fine print on an incentive because *rules* often apply. For instance, 0 percent financing is usually for those with perfect credit, so if that doesn't describe you, chances are you aren't getting it. Keep in mind that if it sounds too good to be true, it probably is. Check that ad again. If it still seems like an amazing offer, call the dealership's financing department and ask what the catch is because every deal has one—*especially* in car sales.

New? Used? Which way should you swing?

Whether or not you swing new or used depends on a few factors. First, you might consider what incentives or rebates are available for new cars. Sometimes the new car deal is a bit difficult to turn down, especially if you have new-car envy [a term to describe those who cannot stand when their close friends  one-up them]. **BUT WAIT! There's more!** Other considerations might include the following:

◈ **Trade-in value.** [This is how much cash you can get from the dealer for your current ride, plus how well the car you desire holds its value. Considering that a new car rapidly depreciates in its first three years, buying a used car is often quite appealing to some.]

◈ **Warranties.** [It used to be that warranties were one size fits all—three years or 36,000 miles—but now they come in all shapes and sizes and are available for used cars, too! However, many used cars are often at the tail end of the dealership warranty or have already driven by it, so keep that in mind! In that case, the buyer is left to pay for repair expenses—from taillights to brakes.]

◈ **Repairs and safety features.** [Safety features are another consideration when evaluating the pros and cons of buying a new versus used car. Safety features have continued to improve over the years, and you can expect to find certain common features, like anti-lock brakes. However, it's incredible how car manufacturers keep adding and improving car safety features with items like air bags,

QUESTION: I decided to lease a great SUV with all the extras, but now I'm thinking I maybe shouldn't have. The payments are a little harder to make than I thought they would be. Is there anything I can do? — Sam, 23

ANSWER: Oh, Sam! How are you doing? It doesn't sound like you're doing too well, really. You didn't follow your parents' advice and bit off more than you could chew, huh? *Come here, baby!* Let your favorite editors comfort you. We have some good news for you, Sam. There is a way to get out of it! While backing out of a lease can be costly [sorry, baby, but you are usually charged penalties, and it negatively affects your credit], several websites will allow you to transfer your lease. Sites such as www.swaplease.com and

LATCH child seat restraints, and so on. Some features may be more important to you than others, so be sure you add safety to your list of items to think about.]

What's the deal with leasing?

In addition to new or used cars, another option buyers have is to lease a car [it's kind of like renting a car, but not exactly]. Most financial peeps frown on leasing. However, if you make good money, it's definitely a valid option. Now, the benefits of leasing a car are that buyers can usually drive a better car than they could otherwise afford and they can get a new car every three years [you know, vanity]. Also, leasers don't have to worry much about car repairs because they're always driving a new vehicle.

The Good and Bad of Leasing

GOOD! When leasing a car, your payments are less than if you had purchased the car.

BAD! On average you are paying for 50 percent depreciation, plus interest. Though this makes for a low monthly payment, at the end of your lease, you will have no equity on your car, so the cost to buy the vehicle [if you so choose] will be higher.

BAD! On average, dealers will try to get you to buy your leased car for $3,000 to $4,000 more than its market value.

GOOD! Leasing is a great way for first-time buyers or buyers with bad credit to establish good credit because www.leasetrader.com will enable you to make this transfer without all those costly headaches. [Transferring your lease lets you trade your lease in with the dealership or another lessee.] These resources are great for people like you who committed to a lease that was a bit too expensive for their budget, as well as for people who have perhaps run into some financial difficulties, like losing a job. Hope this helps!

Tootles.

>>The editors

PS: Send us your comments and questions at WeLoveWritingForMatthew@yahoo.com.

sometimes leasing is the only way a dealership will finance you.

BAD! Leasing often—not always—requires a big down payment.

GOOD! Leasing also usually includes a warranty from the dealership, so you don't have to worry about costly repairs on your vehicle.

BAD! A BIG disadvantage of leasing is that there are mileage limits, and additional fees might occur when the vehicle is returned.

EXTRA!!! Be aware of clauses, such as those regarding accidents, causing termination. You may have to terminate your lease contract but still pay the remaining balance if you get in an accident. [😠 Yeah, this sucks!]

Where to buy?
[10 is good/1 is not so good]

Overall score	Best deal?	Can I test-drive?	Friendly atmo-sphere?	Free coffee?	Negotiable?	Selection?
Dealership 7	You can get some pretty good deals!	Oh, yeah! Do it!	Yeah, but it's often a little like *The Stepford Wives*!	Yep.	Depends on your credit.	Pretty good.
eBay 7.5	Great deals. But you could get cheated, too!	Um, no, not so much!	Well, if you like being friendly over e-mail, then yeah!	Nope.	Depends on the seller.	From BMWs to junkers!
From a friend 6.5	Good deal is possible, but you can lose friendships this way, too.	You probably already have.	Yeah, you're friends, silly!	Probably not!	Depends on the friendship.	Umm, no.
Mom and Dad 10 — if it's free	It's your mom!	You can even run errands.	This depends on your mom and dad.	Maxwell House, baby!	Depends on relationship.	Not so much.

Best advice about car buying: Take your time!

The best advice about buying a car my father ever gave me was to take my time. When you're in the market for a new car, you're apt to get in a hurry. Why? Because you're really excited, and when you're really excited, you're apt to make rash decisions, forget about doing research, and take the first deal that sounds good! So even before you begin the process of car buying, make sure you plan to take your time and find the best deal you can.

Six Questions with a Former Car Salesman!

While twenty-eight-year-old James Dixen was getting his masters in theology and youth development, he sold cars as a way to pay for college. I asked the current youth pastor for a little insight on those annoying car salespeople.

MPT: Hey, James! What kind of cars did you sell? Anything cool like Jaguars? Or BMWs?

JAMES: Ha ha! No. I sold cars at a Ford dealership. It wasn't too bad. The worst part of my job was the dress code — I had to wear a tie every day.

MPT: Okay, so you probably saw car buyers make a bunch of mistakes, right? Well, what mistake did you see people making most often?

JAMES: You know, the worst thing you can do is to come into a car dealership not knowing what you want. If you do that, you're apt to get screwed. So before you walk onto a car lot, know what you're interested in and be as detailed as you can possibly be. You don't want a car dealer telling you what you want!

MPT: Why do most car salespeople get fat? Do they sit around eating those "customer doughnuts" all day long?

JAMES: [Laughs] No! Well, I didn't. But you know, I did gain ten pounds working there.

MPT: What should a car buyer do when he or she is feeling pressure to buy?

JAMES: Just tell the person you're not ready to make the decision. In fact, my advice would be to NEVER make a decision to buy a car on the spot. All those "It might not be here tomorrow" kind of excuses are a bunch a crap. And honestly, if it's not there tomorrow, it probably wasn't supposed to happen for you. Remember, *you're* in control when you buy a car. Car salespeople are taught to take control of a person's buying experience, so you have to be mentally prepared to own your experience.

MPT: So, James, what's the worst line you ever used to try to get someone to buy a car?

JAMES: Eh, well, I wasn't too much of a line user, but I did go out on a date with a car buyer once. She told me she'd buy if I took her out. So I did. Yeah, needless to say, the date didn't work out, but the commission on my sale sure did.

MPT: So you're a player?

JAMES: Yeah, pretty much.

MPT: And you call yourself a man of God.

JAMES: *Hey, I have the degree to prove it!*

Almost Everything You Need to Know About Buying a House!

YAY!!!!

I just felt like shouting for a moment. Sometimes when I'm writing I need to yell once in a while — just to stay sane. It can get rather frazzling being cooped up inside my house all day writing, researching, talking to the birds that chirp just outside my window, and writing some more.

So once in a while I do need to get loud and rambunctious.

And you can do that when you're inside square footage that you own [or are in the process of owning]. There's something very nice about calling a building or a portion of a building or a piece of property your own. You can run around naked in a building that's your own. Of course, you can actually run around naked in any building, just not legally.

Owning [or should I say stewarding] a home has a lot of privileges. But the process of owning/stewarding a home can be overwhelming. In fact, a British study on stress found that 44 percent of those surveyed ranked house buying the number one most stressful event they had endured.[2]

For most of my life, I've heard married couples confess that house buying was one of the most difficult periods of their marriage. And having gone through the process myself, I can attest to the fact that it is indeed anxiety ridden.

A lot is involved in buying a home. And it's a process that many of us go into without truly knowing what we're doing. Or some of us resist the process altogether because we're clueless about how to do it.

Consider these statements from twentysomethings:

- ※ "I wouldn't know the first thing about buying a house; I'm glad I'm poor." —*Ashley, 23*
- ※ "I bought a condo when I was twenty-five. I'm glad my father was there to help me; if not, I would have signed a horrible deal." —*Geoff, 27*
- ※ "I'm not ready to buy a house just yet. I like the flexibility of renting. And hopefully my future husband will know what the heck he's doing." —*Jenna, 24*

Unless you're filthy rich [and are able to pay cash for your new home], more than likely you'll end up having a mortgage on your new home. Well, some of you are pretty darn clueless [see quotes from other twentysomethings on page 149] about the ins and outs of a home mortgage. So I thought it might be important to offer you a little guide to the basic mortgage lingo. Like I mentioned in section 2, money stuff has a language all its own, and mortgages are no different!

- **Mortgage.** This is a loan from a bank or other type of lender that will allow you to purchase a home or property. Of course, you have to pay this money back *with interest.*

- **Principal.** The principal is the *amount* of money you'll be borrowing.

- **Bi-weekly mortgage.** This is an arrangement where you pay twice a month versus once a month. You should talk to your bank about how this can save you LOTS of money on interest!

- **Loan's term.** The amount of time you're given to pay back your loan in monthly installments. [But if you win the lottery, you can pay this back in one lump sum!]

- **Amortization.** This is a really big word that describes how your monthly installment gets divided between the principal of the loan and the interest you owe the lender. Basically, at the beginning of your loan's term, most of your monthly payments go toward the interest of the loan. [The bank wants its money first!] Toward the end of your loan, most of the money you owe goes directly toward the loan's principal!

- **Title.** A legal document showing ownership of property.

- **Appraisal.** This little word describes a detailed analysis by a housing professional that gives you an estimate on the current fair market value of your house.

- **Escrow.** This is an account created by the bank or lender for YOU so they can pay for things like property taxes and house insurance on your behalf.

✿ Lien. Umm, this usually isn't a good thing because it's a claim against your property that must be paid when it's sold! Anything from unpaid taxes to late car payments can put a lien on your home.

✿ Contingency. This is basically a stipulation that must be met before a contract is legit.

THE SCARY REALITY OF A MORTGAGE

At forbeginners.info, they offer this little chart to help you understand how *amortization* works! So you're borrowing $100,000 at 7 percent interest to buy a home. Let's pretend your monthly payments are $665; here's how your payments would be split up if you were to pay back the loan in its entirety in 360 payments [thirty years]![3]

Payment	Amount	Interest	Principal	Loan balance
First payment	$665	$583	$82	$99,918
At 5 years	$665	$550	$115	$94,132
At 10 years	$665	$501	$164	$85,812
At 20 years	$665	$336	$329	$57,300
Last payment	$665	$4	$661	$0

Something you should know! Okay, so you paid off the loan! Good job. You were thirty when you began paying this sucker back, and now you're sixty! Wow. Well, you might want to know that you've paid the bank an additional $139,509! Yeah, that means you've paid the bank a whopping $239,509! Makes you want to buy a house, huh?

Home-Buying Advice from an Expert

If I ever buy another house, I'm calling Nancy Hubbell for her advice. She's the mom of one of my best friends, and she knows more about home buying than anybody I know. [And despite being a mom, Ms. Hubbell has awesome fashion sense.] I know why people trust her with their home buying. Ms. Hubbell's twenty-some years of experience as a Realtor have led to her becoming one of the most respected in her community. To her, it's a joy and blessing that most of her business comes from past clients and referrals. In this conversation, Ms. Hubbell explains the process of buying a house.

MPT: Ms. Hubbell, how does one qualify for a mortgage? And how does someone know what type of mortgage would be best for him or her?

MS. HUBBELL: You may contact the lender [*bank, credit union — any place you're able to borrow money from*] with whom you do business, requesting their rates and mortgage programs. You may check online for rates and mortgages, or your Realtor may refer you to two or three different lenders. Once you decide on the lender, they can prepare a prequalification letter, which is based on your income/debt ratio, stating the amount and terms of the mortgage for which you qualify. They can also prepare a preapproval letter that requires credit, employment verification, and availability of funds for the down payment and closing costs.

The prequalification takes just one to two hours, and the preapproval five to seven days. But make sure you *do not* give out your social security number or authorize anyone to check your credit until you have selected the lender. Some lenders may say that your credit score could have an impact on the interest rate you get or type of mortgage for which you qualify. That is true. However, each time a potential creditor makes an inquiry on your credit, it can reduce your credit score. Those inquiries usually take ninety days to be expunged from your credit report.

MPT: How much money does one need for a down payment and other costs?

MS. HUBBELL: The funds you need for the down payment and closing costs may vary with the type of mortgage you choose. The lender is required by law to give you a good-faith estimate of all your costs. You must check with your Realtor regarding any real estate costs not directly associated with the mortgage — like a home warranty, a broker processing fee, or inspection fees. [*A good rule of thumb is this: You should have at least 10 to 20 percent of a home's total cost.*]

MPT: Now, is it okay if a family member or friend offers money toward a down payment and other expenses?

MS. HUBBELL: In many cases a parent or grandparent can contribute funds to you and usually writes a gift letter stating that the funds do not need to be repaid. Even if they do have to be repaid, by having the letter, this will not be considered a loan and be factored into your debt ratio. Friends are typically not invited to participate.

MPT: Does anyone in the real estate business represent or work for the home buyer? Or do I need an attorney?

MS. HUBBELL: Realtors in most states have agency relationships with sellers and purchasers. One of your Realtor's responsibilities is to discuss with you at the very beginning of your working relationship the forms of agency. In most cases the Realtor working with you will be a buyer broker, working on your behalf. There are, however, some exceptions to this rule [ask your Realtor to explain these]. Some states require an attorney to handle the transaction once the price and terms have been negotiated. Other states allow the Realtor and title company to process all documents and conduct the closing. One item you may want an attorney to review is the title commitment to be certain that the title is clear and can be passed to you without any concerns.

MPT: What should a buyer take into consideration when choosing the best area in the city/community?

MS. HUBBELL: That's a good question. You know the old saying, "Everything comes down to LOCATION, LOCATION, LOCATION!" A few things you should consider are access to expressways and proximity to schools, churches, shopping, and recreation. The potential for growth in the community and the appreciation of property, along with the quality of the school district, are very important considerations when choosing a town or neighborhood within the town, too. Remember, this is usually a substantial investment, and you would want a good return when it comes time to sell.

MPT: How does one decide what type of housing to purchase?

MS. HUBBELL: I think this really depends a great deal on your lifestyle and the continued investment required in the property after the purchase — in other words, association fees and how much maintenance you want to do yourself or can afford to pay someone else to do. For instance, if you purchase brand-new, which requires that you put in the landscaping, deck, patio, window treatments, and so on, and you need to resell in a short time, depending on the market conditions, you may not be able to get back all you've invested. Be careful also of buying a fixer-upper without having precise estimates on the fixes, particularly if you cannot do the work yourself.

MPT: How does one find out if the property he or she wants is in good condition? In other words, if the structure, mechanicals, electrical/ plumbing systems, well and septic [*for the country folk*], appliances, and radon levels are up to par? What about any zoning issues?

MS. HUBBELL: In most states the seller is required to complete a lengthy form called the seller's disclosure that asks him or her to answer several questions pertaining to these and other items, like property shared in common [pools, parks, and the like], age of roof, environmental issues, and so on. One caution: The seller's statement is not a guarantee or warranty of the condition of the property. Most Realtors highly recommend you conduct a contractor's inspection of the home. This is a contingency of the purchase, at your expense, and takes two to four hours. Your Realtor can suggest two to three inspectors from whom you can choose. Also, some sellers will provide, or you can purchase, a home warranty that is like an insurance policy, covering certain items in the home for one year after the closing. It is your Realtor's responsibility to inform you of all suggested testing and any other pertinent details, such as zoning/developing in the area.

MPT: How do I know if there are deed restrictions that govern what I can and can't do in the neighborhood?

MS. HUBBELL: Your Realtor will [or should] know if there are restrictions. If the home has an association, is a condo, or is in a neighborhood that owns any property in common [in other words, pool, playground, and so forth], there are usually rules. I always provide my purchasers with a copy of the restrictions and conditions on the purchase agreement five to seven days in advance so they can review and accept the restrictions. This is also the time to learn about any association dues/fees. Some are mandatory, in particular if the roads are private and must be maintained by the association or if there are amenities owned in common. If they are not paid, the association can place a lien on your property until they are paid, or, in some cases, they may do the work, such as mow the lawn, and bill you for the service. It's always wise to check the terms of insurance that cover common elements. Occasionally, some fees are voluntary, such as for planting flowers at an entry to the neighborhood.

MPT: How does a buyer know how much to offer to pay for the property?

MS. HUBBELL: As a buyer broker, your Realtor is able to provide for you comparables. If the Realtor does not offer to do this for you and you are not knowledgeable about property values in the area, please request that they be provided. Comparables include details regarding similar properties that are currently on the market. More important, they provide information on the asking and final sale price of similar properties, along with the time the properties had been on the market prior to selling. With recent sales data, you can compare square footage, number of bedrooms/baths, garage, lot size, and other amenities of the properties that have sold. The ratio of asking to sales price and the market time will help you determine general market conditions. In other words, you can learn if the properties are appreciating well and selling in a favorable time period. Is the market more stable with lower appreciation? Or is the market really soft with no growth, declining values, and longer selling periods? [*These are important things to consider — Ms. Hubbell says so!*]

One more thing, Matthew! This would also be a good time to have your Realtor give you the public tax record on the property so you can see the SEV [state equalized value — when doubled, it equals what the state thinks the property is worth; this can vary 10 to 20 percent +/-]. The SEV, or in some states the taxable value, shows the value on which the property taxes are based. In most areas, at the time of sale the taxing authority can increase the SEV or taxable value to half of the sales price. When multiplied by the mileage rate, this will give you the approximate new property tax amount. If some homes have not been sold for a long time, they can have a very low taxable value, but when the taxable value is adjusted to reflect the new sales price, you can have a substantial increase in the taxes that could affect how well you qualify for the mortgage. All this information should help you in determining a fair purchase price, but do expect some negotiating.

MPT: What does one need to make an offer to purchase property?

MS. HUBBELL: Your Realtor will prepare all the documents with the details of your offer — price, terms, and any contingencies — and you will need to provide an earnest money deposit — a check, usually $1,000 or more depending on what is customary in your area. The deposit is a good-faith statement on your part to indicate to the seller that you are serious. Usually the deposit is refundable if the offer cannot be negotiated or if there are any contingencies on the offer that cannot be met by you or the seller. When the agreement is negotiated, the EMD is deposited in an escrow account with your Realtor's broker. When all contingencies are satisfied and you are ready to close the sale, your deposit is applied toward your purchasing costs as a credit to you.

MPT: What do you do after all the contingencies are satisfied?

MS. HUBBELL: You wait. This is the time when your lender is doing the appraisal [*you should be able to receive a copy of this*] and ordering the mortgage survey [*not a stake survey with boundary markers – ask your Realtor*] and the title company is searching the registrar of deeds for all recordings on the property, preparing the title commitment [*these policies vary, so again, talk to your Realtor*], and preparing all the documents needed for the closing. It would be at this time, after you've received a copy of the title commitment and before the closing, that you may want an attorney's review.

Your House-Buying Checklist!

❑ Learn the mortgage process!
- ■ Only look into what you can afford. [⇨ *Your daddy's been telling you this for years!*]
- ■ Pay off small debts before you apply. [⇨ *Even if your credit card balance is only $300, get rid of it before you apply!*]
- ■ Don't forget about closing costs.
- ■ Compare lenders. [⇨ *Try LendingTree.com.*]

- Consider a fifteen- to twenty-year term rather than a thirty-year term. [⇨ *Saves you a ton of money!*]

☐ Get preapproved! [⇨ *Or at least begin the process!*]

☐ Check out this site: http://www.ourfamilyplace.com/homebuyer/timeline.html. [⇨ *You'll find a basic buying-a-house timeline.*]

☐ Make your home budget *before* you decide to buy a new home! [⇨ *You need to know what you can afford.*]

☐ Find a buying agent you trust! [⇨ *Talk to family or friends and ask them who they used when they purchased their last house.*]

☐ Familiarize yourself with the different types of houses. [⇨ *You know, condos, single-family homes, mansions, high-rise apartments, and so on.*]

☐ Go house hunting! [⇨ *Not sure I need to explain what this means.*]

☐ Be informed on how to negotiate a good price. [⇨ *Talk to your Realtor, friends, and family and find out the temperature of the market in your area.*]

☐ Plan to have your new home inspected. [⇨ *This will protect you in the long run!!! So just do it!*]

☐ Think about getting a house warranty and insurance. [⇨ *Talk to your Realtor about the benefits!*]

☐ Schedule a lawyer or agent for the closing. [⇨ *He or she will make the contract process a lot simpler!*]

☐ Do a final walk-through of your new home. [⇨ *You want

to make sure everything is to your liking! So make sure you do this!]

❑ CLOSING MEETING!!! [➪ *This is where you hand over the big check!*]

❑ Move in. [➪ *Hang up a picture or two.*]

A Few Things You Need to Know About Investing Your Money

Have you ever seen a senior citizen driving a BMW convertible? Sure, you have. And you've probably also seen a few of those BMW-driving senior citizens sporting one of those cool bumper stickers that reads, "I am spending my children's inheritance."

That bumper sticker always makes me smile. Sure, it smacks of cockiness and self-absorption, but I still smile. Now, hopefully you won't be as self-consumed as some of the old farts who drive up and down our highways today.

Most of us aren't fortunate enough to have a million-dollar trust fund waiting for us [*heck, most of us will probably be lucky to receive our mother's really cool floral-patterned china tea set or our dad's pocket watch or his favorite golf clubs*]. As you have probably realized, the days of getting rich off your parents' investments are long gone [*again, for most of us*]. So it's imperative that we invest a part of what we make now to ensure our ability to live generous lives when we're older.

Did you know that today's experts say that we need to have a minimum of $1 million in a retirement package in order to live comfortably and generously in our older years? *Umm, that's a lot of cash!* And, unfortunately, that dollar figure is increasing rapidly as the years pass by.

Believe me, I'm not trying to scare you into investing or sound like I'm promoting a get-rich-quick scheme. I'm not. Investing is about taking what God gives each of us and making the most of it so we are able to continue giving abundantly to his work [and, not to mention, provide for our families] while we're here on earth.

Think back to the parable of the ten talents (see Luke 19:11-27). Jesus' story went a little something like this: There were ten servants that were each given ten talents by their master. After giving his servants their talents, the master then went on a vacation to some crazy-nice vacation spot in Cabo.

The servants all had the same amount of time and unlimited potential to grow their master's money while he was away. As Jesus explained, one servant was a risk taker. He invested in the early 1990s dot-com stocks and got out before they crashed. [*Not really, but you get the point!*] He doubled his master's money in no time! [*Cheers for the first servant!*] A second servant was a bit more moderate in his investing habits, choosing to invest in government bonds. But despite being a bit conservative, he was able to garner a 50 percent return on his talent! [*Good job, second servant!*] A third servant was a "mattress stuffer" and decided to bury his master's money in the ground because he feared he might lose the money entrusted to him. [*The third servant was naughty!*]

Now, when the master returned, he brought in his financial planners and asked for their portfolio prospectuses. The first servant boldly told of how his risky investing had produced a double return. The master expressed his favor with the servant and gave him the money he had invested! The same was done for the moderate-investing servant. But the third servant was given a verbal beating by the master for his lack of financial wisdom and his lack of effort to build on the foundation the master had set up for him.

So what's the moral of the story? INVEST! INVEST! INVEST! Or at least be wise in how you handle the Master's money.

Investing 101

[because most of us can only
handle the beginning stuff]

Okay, so here's the thing: Opportunities for investing sometimes feel like you're standing at the counter at Baskin-Robbins.
You know, *lots of flavors!* With so many ice cream flavors available, it's sort of difficult picking one or two that are guaranteed
to give your taste buds the biggest bang for their buck.

The sidebar below gives one twentysomething's story about
investing toward his retirement.

To 401k or Not to 401k? — That's Not Really the Question
[by David Banks]

When I began working, I was fortunate enough to land a job where the company offered a 401k program. I thought, *Wow, this is a cool concept — I tell my
company to take 5 percent of my income each pay period and place it into an
account that will make me money.*

So that's what I did. Okay, so it was great, but I didn't think I could pay my
bills with *100 percent* of my income, let alone 95 percent. I sought the advice of
a man who was not extremely wealthy but had the financial wisdom only gained
from years of experience. He told me that I should find out if my company offered
to match my investment in the 401k plan. I researched and discovered that they
would match my investment — up to 6 percent of my salary. I reported back to
my mentor, and he said this 6 percent matching fund was like getting a raise. He
said to invest at least 6 percent to get the entire matching funds. He said I would
hardly miss the income in the first few months of investing. I followed his advice,
and within three years my 401k was over $13,000.

You're probably wondering if there's a secret formula to guarantee financial security, huh? Umm, not really. However, there are some basic things you can do to begin learning the ins and outs of investing wisely. Here are some simple ideas to get you started!

✷ **Talk to your human resources department!** Like I mentioned in the last section, have a conversation with your HR department to find out your options regarding retirement at the company you work for. Learn where your money is being invested and what the penalties are if you withdraw from it too soon. One thing you will want to discuss with them is the company's 401k plan!

> ▶ **401k.** These investments are normally tied to your employment, and usually companies will match a portion of your investment. This is a before-tax investment that comes out of your gross income. If your company offers this benefit, this is a program you simply must participate in. Be patient; this is not an overnight payoff.

✷ **Set up a meeting with a financial counselor!** A financial counselor can look at your financial situation and help you devise an investment plan that is right for you. Talk to this person about your goals *and* your limitations. When you meet, make sure he or she explains the benefits of a Roth IRA.

▶ **Roth IRA.** If you are young, this option has great appeal. The simple explanation of this investment is that the money you invest is money that comes out of your net income — or money that you have already paid taxes on. Here is the best part: No matter how much your investment grows, you will never pay taxes on that money again.

⋮ **Take a bite out of the stock market yourself!** Although both a 401k and a Roth IRA will be partly made up of stocks, the stock market offers great potential in making the most of your money. One college professor told me that he would buy one hundred shares of stock in any company that he used. So the next time you shop at Wal-Mart or drink a Coke, think of the money you would be making if you owned a portion of those companies.

⋮ **Know this: This will take time!** Investing takes a great deal of discipline and a continued commitment to a program.

A consistent approach to investing will lead to *a greater chance of* financial security for you and your family. However, that financial security takes years to develop, so don't think that you will see huge returns on your investments overnight.

The Lowdown on Your Investment Options and Their Associated Risks

Option	What is it?	Risk?	When will you see a return?	Skill level?
401k	This is a long-term, before-tax investment, usually through your employer. Some employers will match the funds you invest.	There are usually three levels of risk to this investment: low, medium, and high. Most plans will have a moderate track, which has a middle-of-the-road risk factor.	These plans normally have an age limit you must meet before you can collect. The normal age is sixty.	You can do well with no experience by following the charts provided by the investing agency. Most plans will also have administrators that will be able to assist you.
Roth IRA	This is a long-term, after-tax investment. The advantage to this investment is that regardless of how much you make, you will never pay taxes on the money again.	As with the 401k, there are low-, medium-, and high-risk tracks to the Roth IRA.	Again, the normal age is sixty.	Hint: Same as 401k! That saves me from having to write it again.
Real estate	This is simple. Be like Donald Trump and buy property, improve it, and sell it to make a profit.	This has a high risk due to fluctuating markets.	You could see a return on your investment overnight. I have seen people buy property one day and sell it the next to make a small profit. It's high risk, but you could see high returns.	Unlike the late-night paid commercials, this option takes a lot of skill. To be successful, one must have some knowledge of the real-estate markets, construction, and real-estate sales.

Option	What is it?	Risk?	When will you see a return?	Skill level?
Stocks	This investment is the Dow Jones and NASDAQ.	There are different levels of risk with this investment. The risk is determined by the company you buy stock in. Companies like IBM are low-risk, steady companies. Technology companies like the dot-coms are high risk.	Some people day-trade and see returns within minutes. To ensure success, take a ten-year approach to this investment. The stock market has proven to be the surest of all investments over a ten-year period.	Many companies offer you the tools to invest on your own. Be careful with this investment and seek advice from experienced financial advisers.
Mutual funds	Mutual funds are combinations of stock and government bonds. This investment diversifies your money over many companies, giving you a return based on average performances of these companies.	Can be risky, but it's normally only moderate — but you can choose higher or lower risk if you desire.	This is another long-term investment. Look for a fifteen- to thirty-year plan for the best return.	Trust the pros with this one. Follow the charts provided by your agency and be consistent.
Bonds	This investment consists of government bonds, Treasury bonds, and so on.	This is a low-risk investment due to the steadiness of the government. This investment will usually produce a low return, around 5 percent.	This investment is slow but steady. Most bonds will have a maturity date that is more than five years away.	Little or no skill is needed here. Pick a bond and wait till it matures. Do not expect to get really rich here, but at least you won't lose your shorts either.

Option	What is it?	Risk?	When will you see a return?	Skill level?
Certificates of deposit (CDs)	This investment is offered by your local bank. It is a savings account that pays a bit more interest but has certain terms you must meet before you can access your money.	This investment is very low risk. You lock in for a certain rate, usually 4 to 5 percent, and a term of three to ten years. Wait for the time to elapse and collect your interest.	You will know the time it will take to get a return by the terms of the CD.	None. Ask your bank what they offer and make your choice.

Okay, so this section was a bit long. However, I do believe it was filled with lots of good information for all of us to consider. Are you beginning to feel the power of financial wisdom yet?

No?!?

Maybe I'm expecting too much from my writing. No, really, I probably am. I'm a writer, and we writers sometimes think of our content as way too influential.

The Language of Money

[a few translations of the word]

⇨ In English: money
⇨ In Spanish: *dinero*
⇨ In French: *argent*
⇨ In German and Dutch: *geld*
⇨ In Italian: *denaro*
⇨ In Portuguese: *dinheiro*
⇨ In Norwegian: *penger*
⇨ In "simple" Chinese: 钱 [Yeah, try to pronounce that!]

So thanks for the dose of humility. I probably needed it. No, it's okay, really! While the editors write this next section, I'm going to go call my therapist and see if he can talk me down from this "ledge" you've just put me on. It's okay; I'll survive.

So while I'm in counseling, read this next section about getting out of credit card debt. You will love it!

The Credit Card

[the editors of *What You Didn't Learn from Your Parents About Money* help you get out of debt]

Debt is the worst poverty.

— Thomas Fuller

[If Thomas Fuller had lived in modern Sudan, I believe his quote would be different.]

Hello! It's us, the editors! You might know us from such places as *What You Didn't Learn from Your Parents About Sex, What You Didn't Learn from Your Parents About Christianity,* and *What You Didn't Learn from Your Parents About Politics*! Yeah, throughout this series, Matthew has limited us to answering a few questions and providing a little bit of commentary. Between you and us, Matthew's a little bit of a literary hog. He writes EVERYTHING! For some reason he seems to think we're not capable of writing an entire section in one of his books. So he always confines us to answering silly questions. Oh, don't get us wrong; we do love answering questions, but it gets a little old from time to time.

However, things have changed. Finally, after a good month of being on our knees *begging* Matthew to give us a chance at writing a full section, he came to his book-writing senses and decided to let us steer the wheel on this section about all things credit cards—but most important, about getting out of *credit card debt.*

So here we are writing our first complete section of the series. And *you should be thanking the good Lord!* Because unlike much of this book, where the content tends to be dryer than an

Arizona cactus on the last Tuesday afternoon of the summer, this section will actually be a lot of fun to read. Well, that's our goal anyway. I mean, Matthew did give us the most disheartening part of money—*debt*.

I think we're about to officially get started! But before we do, we have a few rules you must follow. Ordinarily we're not big fans of rules, but that changed when Matthew began giving us control.

We *love* having control. It's kind of gone to our heads a bit. So now we want our bodies morphed into one big, fat ripoff of Oprah. And since Oprah loves sharing her rules, we thought we should open with a rule or two of our own.

Here we go! [Of course, Matthew's telling us to hurry our butts along; he thinks we're being long-winded. *Obviously he hasn't read his own section 4!*]

RULE #1: No Christianese! Nothing gets our big ole Oprah panties in a wad faster than *Christianese*. So while you're reading this section, can you please refrain from using words like *victory*, *doctrine*, *freedom in Christ*, and *Habakkuk*? And while we're at it, can you also please avoid [*like a plague of Egypt!*] reciting all *Seinfeld* colloquialisms, stupid movie quotes, and any lyric by Nelly [*we're so over Nelly*].

Okay, that's the only rule; everything else we can/will tolerate. We're really nice controllers, aren't we?

Now let's get to talking about the topic at hand.

THE CREDIT CARD!

Ah, the credit card — one of the world's most treasured creations. Yes, we know how delighted you get when that thin piece of colored plastic sits between your thumb and index finger. Yeah, we've been there, honey; we used to be credit card lovers, too. We know all about the power of the *swipe*!

Swipe this.

And *swipe* that. [On a side note, have you ever been "credit carded"? Oh, we have. When we were in high school, these two boys would always come up behind us and slide their flat palms up our butt cheeks. It was very embarrassing. But now we're married, so we think it's fun!!]

We *know* the swipe is as alluring as Brad Pitt [😋 *yum*] in that scene from *Thelma & Louise*. Yeah, you guys might not know what scene we're talking about, but every lady reading this section is swooning a bit.

But just like Brad became a lot less scrumptious when he left Jen for Angelina, credit cards became a thorn in our backsides when they turned our financial situations into something resembling a Ben Affleck movie. And other than *Good Will Hunting*, you know how disastrous movies starring Ben Affleck have been, right?

Need we mention *Surviving Christmas*, *Jersey Girl*, or *Paycheck*? Yeah, you get our point.

Yep, that's the shape our financial lifestyles were in prior to us giving up credit cards.

As you read in section 3, Matthew discussed a little bit about his own credit card woes. But we've got the scoop on how bad his situation actually was, and between you and us, it was like *Gigli*. You see, Matthew didn't really tell you the whole story. So don't tell him we've gone and divulged his little secret. But he got himself into a heap of credit card debt. We're talking nearly $20,000 worth of credit card debt.

Yes, $20,000! Now you see why we should have been writing this book all along, huh?

We'll let that rather large figure sink in a bit.

Yep, that was the total of his three credit cards when he got married in October 2004. [*Ha ha! His poor wife.*] Each of the three cards [a Capital One Visa, a Bank of America MasterCard, and an American Express Blue Card, *which was a very cool-looking card*, we might add] were all maxed out. Yep, maxed out!

But guess what? There's good news to report, sweeties! Within one year and nine months of his wedding bells ringing, Matthew had whittled that credit card debt down to zero. *Yes, he and his wife had managed to completely eliminate their bad debt.*

Seems impossible, huh?

BUT GUESS WHAT? YOU CAN DO IT, TOO!

It just takes discipline. *And, of course, some money.*

Now, we're not going to tell you every dirty detail about how Matthew and Jessica got out of their financial bind, but we are going to offer you the best wisdom we know about how *you* can get rid of that small, large, or humungous debt you're living under.

Yeah, we know all about what it feels like living under a pile of debt. But can you just imagine living life without the financial stress of that big ole debt hanging over your head? Ah, now, that's how we spell relief!

Like Matthew [and all of the guest interviewees] have said throughout this book, healthy and godly financial living begins with realizing that all of us are stewards [*not owners*] of God's money. And as stewards, we're called to live without *bad debt*. Why? Because spending money that has not been put in our care is wrong.

The Editors' Guide to Losing That Bad Credit Card Debt

First and foremost, you'd better learn this:
ANY AND ALL CREDIT CARD DEBT IS BAD!

Yep, that's what we said. We know this seems a bit drastic to some of you. But think of it like this: When you're in debt to someone else, it's kind of like putting yourself in financial slavery [*and who likes slavery of any kind?*]. Whether you've got $500 sitting on your MasterCard or you've got $5,000, honey, you are enslaved [chained up] to Madame MasterCard until you pay that biddy off.

[Okay, story time!]

Why should you hate debt? Consider this story about our friend Jenny.

Our friend Jenny [she's twenty-four] was $8,500 in debt when she came to see us. Poor Jenny was depressed when she walked through our door. She'd been on a financial slope for nearly five years—shopping for furniture, buying clothes, and scrapbooking were problems for her. Every time she'd try to pull herself out of financial trouble, she'd end up giving up or getting behind on payments or only paying the minimum. She's had a dickens of a time trying to get out of debt. When she came to see us, we figured out that in the last five years, she'd paid the credit card company $4,300. But due to her high interest, she'd only put $900 toward her actual balance.

Like we said, Jenny was financially depressed. And, honey, we see this stuff all the time. Debt doesn't just affect you financially; it affects you spiritually, emotionally, and mentally! Why? Because when you're in debt, you often feel like you're in a big hole you can't possibly dig out of.

Jenny's still working on getting out of that hole. But we're confident that she'll do it.

[Story time is complete!]

So, first, before you can even begin to get out of credit card debt [*or any kind of debt, really, but especially credit card debt!*], you have to get it through that thick skull of yours that any *credit card debt* is bad. You have to hate it. Credit card debt should make you feel similar to how smelling spoiled spilled milk in the backseat of a hot car makes you feel — nauseous!

More than likely, if you're not ready to become nauseous, you're not ready to get out of credit card debt. Now, we don't want any of you sticking your finger down your throat in hopes of forcing a dry heave. But it would be nice if you were to ask God to give you a little hatred toward anything that is going to jeopardize your financial well-being.

You have to become very comfortable with the word *NO*!

Say it! Say the word *no*.

We can't hear you!

SAY IT LOUDLY! Like this:

NO!!!!!!

Now try it again! This time make your neighbors hear it.

Here's the deal, sweetheart: If you want to get out of debt, you're going have to say no *a lot*. And believe us, it's going to be difficult. We still haven't mastered it to perfection. But we say it a lot more *now* than we did when we were sitting in our own financial stench.

When do you have to say NO?

Okay, we'll tell you.

When a friend of yours calls and asks you to go to the movies and you don't have the cash to pay for the movie . . . you say, *"NO! I can't go!"*

When you see a commercial for a brand-new iPod component you've been lusting after for months . . . you say to yourself, *"Self, NO!!!!!!!! You can't always have what you want!"*

When you hear that Gap is having a *huge* sale and the only "money" you have is a credit card . . . *you say, well, you know what you say, right?*

NO!!!!!!

Wow, you're a fast learner! We are very proud and happy editors right now. Okay, you've heard our advice about *hating* credit card debt, and you've listened to us rant about the importance of a good *NO!*, but now it's time for the true test of whether or not you're ready to get rid of your debt....

Get some scissors!

Yep, you totally know where we're going with this one, huh? And you are right. Cut that little piece of plastic [or all five of those little pieces of plastic] into itsy-bitsy pieces. Be done with it/them. Let all of those little pieces die a slow death at the bottom of the nearest trash can.

Write a letter! You like writing letters, right?

Okay, now we think you should write each of your credit card companies a letter telling them that you're closing your account. Don't do this over the phone. [They'll try to stop you from doing it — they'll offer you a whole bunch of great deals! Don't fall for them.] You should always do this in writing because you want to have a record of when you cancelled

your card. And make sure you keep a copy of the letter for your personal records.

When the credit card company has processed your request, you will get a letter in the mail letting you know that your account has been cancelled. Keep that letter.

Now, this is where it gets tricky again. . . .

Gather all of your credit card* statements.

Are you still with us? Are you learning what it means to hate debt? Are you practicing your best *NO*? Are you finishing up those letters to your credit card companies? Okay, so when you've gathered together all of those important documents, put them in order from *smallest debt* to *largest debt*! Don't complicate this, people. Yes, it's as simple as it sounds!

For example, one of our close friends, Mitch, came to us for some advice. When we met, Mitch had the following outstanding debt:

If you would like, you can include all of your debt in this part—school debt, car loan, anything you've financed for your home, and so on.

- Sears card: $567
- Visa card: $2,404
- American Express card: $5,672
- College: $12,132
- Car: $15,307

As you can see, we've listed Mitch's debt from the lowest amount to the highest amount.

**[Okay, now let's take a short break!
Read the following interview!]**

The Editors Interview Keith, a Guy Who Sees a Lot of Debt!

We *love* Keith Edmondson. If we weren't already married, we'd be on him like Matt Lauer was on an interview with Tom Cruise! Not only is Keith a guy who pursues *passionately* after God, but the guy spends his days [and sometimes his nights] working for Dave Ramsey, helping people out of their financial difficulties. Though this book does feature an interview with Dave, we thought it would be cool to get an *insider's* wisdom on dealing with debt!

EDITORS: Keith, we are so glad you could join us! First off, can you explain in twenty words or less what exactly you do at your job? [We'd let you go on and on about your job, but this is ONLY a two-hundred-and-some-page book.]

KEITH: I advise companies on the best ways to teach their employees better personal money management, and sometimes I facilitate that training. [*Ooh, maybe he could come to our place for a little seminar. Maybe he wears a uniform. . . .*]

EDITORS: You talk a lot about debt, huh?
KEITH: Yes, I do.

EDITORS: So you probably know a lot about credit card companies, right?
KEITH: Sure.

EDITORS: Can we ask you a personal question? What's in YOUR wallet?

KEITH: Two debit cards, $50 cash, and all the receipts for the day, including breakfast at Burger King, that I will put in my budget spreadsheet tonight.

EDITORS: Oh, Keith, that's very smart of you, but do you have any fun? Okay, that was mean. But we want to know, for example, if you are ever tempted by those Capital One commercials [you know, the ones with David Spade and that guy saying no a lot].

KEITH: Never. I ran up a lot of credit card debt in college that took me years to pay off, and I don't want to go down that road again. [*He's perfect, huh!*]

EDITORS: Not even a little?
KEITH: Nope.

EDITORS: So do you think hell is anything like a credit card company?
KEITH: Come on, a credit card company provides a service, kind of like a store that sells large knives to small children as toys. [*Ooh, good analogy! Did Dave tell you that one?*]

EDITORS: So you probably hear a lot of crazy credit card stories. What are the three dumbest reasons you've ever heard people give for why they chose to have a credit card?
KEITH: One, because it had a picture of Mickey Mouse on it. Two, because they got a free T-shirt or two-liter bottle of Coke, which they later realized cost them over $500 in interest payments. Three, because they could save 10 percent at their favorite store, which, again, cost them 19 to 29 percent in interest payments. [*Ouch, we've totally fallen for that free Coke idea. But he's right; it was dumb.*]

EDITORS: Wow. That's pretty intense. Can you give us three adjectives that best explain the damaging effects of credit card debt?
KEITH: Overwhelmed/hopeless, alone, and idiotic. I'm describing the feelings real people often have.

EDITORS: Now, when someone calls you for advice or help, what's the first thing you ask them?

KEITH: Are you looking for a quick fix, or do you really want to make some changes?

EDITORS: Okay, now for some "advice" questions. Are any of those companies who "consolidate your credit card charges into one easy payment" legit? Or are they always bad, dishonest, and apt to screw you in the end?

KEITH: There are a couple of legit companies, but the people who use them are still not addressing the *real* problem, even if the math works out and they're saving money. They don't fix the actual problem, and then they go out and spend more because they now have more money for minimum payments. And a lot of times, their debt goes up!

EDITORS: When you're in debt, those awful phone calls from creditors can be hard to handle. Do you have any advice on what you should and shouldn't say to them?

KEITH: Absolutely. First, familiarize yourself with the laws regarding creditor calls.* If laws are broken you have more ground to stand on. Second, ask them to put everything in writing — they hate this. Third, if you are a person who is petrified by conflict, have a counselor help you with these calls. But in any case, you must communicate with your creditors if you want to get out of the mess. Simply ignoring them will destroy you financially.

---

* These vary by state/providence.

EDITORS: Sometimes creditors get nasty and threaten all kinds of things in order to get you to pay, but legally, aren't there limits to what they can actually do and say?

KEITH: Yes, there are limits. I think talking to a certified financial counselor will help you understand the creditors' rights, as well as your rights. At no time are they ever allowed to use vulgarity, for example. Their goal is to make you so emotionally agitated that you pay them with money you don't have just to make them go away.

EDITORS: Yep, you're right about that; we've dealt with some big meanie-heads over the years. Okay, *new topic*! Are you having fun, Keith?

KEITH: Yes, this is great!

EDITORS: Now, one of the perks of your job is more than likely hearing a lot of success stories. Do you have a favorite story? Give us one that will make us cry!

KEITH: Okay, I have one. I was working a live event in Louisville and things were slow at the moment, so I got to walk around the venue, which never happens. I ran into a woman who had to tell me her story. A year earlier she had been in the psychiatric ward of a local hospital for attempted suicide. This was due to what she believed was a hopeless financial situation. Her two children in their early twenties attended the Dave Ramsey live event, bought a couple of books afterward, and immediately took them to the hospital to their mother. At her children's urgings, she began to read. Over the course of the next year, she paid off $5,000 in debt and put $1,500 in the bank on a limited income. She still had a way to go, but her hope had been restored thanks to the support of her children and a biblically based financial education. It's not about the hundreds or thousands of families we help; it is the individual stories that humble me.

EDITORS: Oh, wow, Keith. Are you married?
KEITH: No. [*Ladies, did you catch that?*]

EDITORS: We need to make something happen; you're just too sweet!
KEITH: [Blushes, laughs]

EDITORS: Okay, last question, Keith! If someone NEVER wants to be in a position to HAVE to call your office [which we believe is a good thing unless she's interested in what you're doing on Friday night!], how can he or she make that happen?
KEITH: Get on a budget, find someone to hold you accountable — for couples, it would be your spouse — and follow the seven steps we teach on getting out of debt and building wealth. It is not rocket science; it is self-discipline and deciding what you want your financial goals to be.

EDITORS: Thank you! We had fun.
KEITH: So did I!

Matthew went a different route for getting out of debt. Though he changed his financial lifestyle drastically by cutting out needless expenses and looked for ways to cut big chunks of money out of his budget, Matthew also consulted the expertise of a debt counselor. Knowing that there are many dishonest debt counselors and consolidators out there in the world, he did tons of research before he decided to use the services of Boston-based DMB Financial [DMBFinance.com]. DMB helped Matthew devise a plan to begin whacking away at his debt! They handled all of the negotiations with his creditors and helped him go from debt-filled to debt-free in less than two years! If you're not the most organized person or if you're being hassled by creditors, hiring the services of a financial counselor might be the right move for you! But before you do, make sure you take these steps:

⇒ **Do research.** You want to make sure the company you use is reputable!

⇒ **Ask for references.** Again, you want to make sure the company is reputable!

⇒ **Ask if they have a law office.** The reputable ones should!

⇒ **Ask how they make their money.** If they are just a company that adds up all of your debt and then offers you another loan, don't bite!

⇒ **Know that if they sound TOO GOOD TO BE TRUE, they probably are.**

DEBT FREE!

The Big Names in Debt-Free Living!

Top names	Who they are	Resources	What identifies them	Where to find more info
Dave Ramsey	Dave is a top name in the financial planning world who has tremendous resources to eliminate debt!	*The Total Money Makeover* and also his daily talk-radio show!	A polished and shiny bald head is Dave's most recognizable feature.	www .daveramsey .com
Larry Burkett	Larry was the most widely known financial guide on Christian radio. He has gone to be with the Lord, but while here his knowledge and advice provided a ton of information to live debt-free.	Debt-free living and seventy-plus books meant to help you live a godly and healthy financial lifestyle.	Larry loved to wear his base-ball cap and bomber jacket.	www.crown .org/larry
Suze Orman	Suze is one of the best-known talking heads on finances in tele-vision. She has been beneficial to the lives of so many people with her vast knowledge and advice on living in a financially responsible manner.	Way too many resources to list. Refer to her website.	Late-night TV shows and that cropped, streaked blonde hair. We always thought blondes had more fun! Don't worry; we're not sure what that last sentence means either.	www .suzeorman.com
Mary Hunt	Mary is going on her fourteenth year with her debt-proof living advice and is syndicated across the country with her "Everyday Cheapskate" column.	Debt-proof living.	We think she's the Martha Stewart of financial plan-ning! But she's nicer!	www .debtproofliving .com

Before you begin tackling your debt, save up an emergency fund.

[a little tip we learned from Dave Ramsey!]

The first thing we told Mitch—you know, the friend we helped find his way out of debt—was to save up $1,000 to $1,500. And truly, that's what you should do. This little stow of cash is for *emergencies*. No doubt when you begin thrashing away at your debt, you're going to run into situations where emergency money is going to be needed, things like doctors' visits, car repairs, and broken appliances. By saving up $1,000 to $1,500, you'll be prepared to pay for all those little unexpected situations.

Dave Ramsey thinks you should keep this fund in the form of cash [for the record, we don't think this is necessary! But we also know that Dave's the *financial man*!].

When you have to dip into this fund, you should *replenish* it again as soon as you are able to!

Begin with the lowest debt amount.

Now, once Mitch saved up his emergency fund, we informed him it was time to begin putting all of his extra cash toward his lowest debt amount. *That's right!* It may seem strange to

A Little Hint from Mitch

So here's a little hint for you! Mitch realized after he did his spending analysis [see section 3] that he would be able to put $303 a month toward wiping out his debt! Of course, each month he was also paying minimum payments of $105 toward his Visa card and $234 toward his American Express card. With his extra $303 a month, it took Mitch only two months to wipe out that Sears credit card debt of $567! On the third month of Mitch's "wipe my debt out" plan, he added that $303 to the $105 he was already paying to Visa and began making $408 payments toward that card. It took Mitch six months to pay off Visa, and now he's working like a fiend to get rid of his American Express card! He added that $408 to his American Express minimum of $234 and is currently paying $642 toward that big debt! Mitch is doing very well! You can totally do this, too.

you, but you should begin with the *lowest* amount! *Why?* Well, we'll tell you:

- By eliminating the lowest amount, you're taking the quickest route toward improving your credit. So we recommend that while you're paying the lowest monthly payment on all of your debts, begin putting *all of your extra cash* toward that lowest debt amount.

- By focusing on the lowest amount, you'll see *progress* and *success* more quickly than you would if you were focusing on the largest amount or tackling several amounts at the same time!

- Organization is the key here! Once you have a plan, you'll feel like Batman and Robin beating up all the bad "debt" guys!

After you've eliminated one, begin slashing another.

Staying motivated is the hardest part of reducing your debt. So every time you win [you win by slashing one of your totals!], throw a mini-party! But then start slashing away on another debt!

In closing, we'd like to offer this disclaimer. When you're dealing with financial issues, it's always good to seek a second opinion. We know that all financial situations are different and are sometimes very complicated, so seeking out the best option for you is extremely important.

But whatever you do, we, the editors, don't think you should accept your debt-filled situation; it's not good to be in debt. Yes, thinking about it probably makes you a wee bit crazy, but *not thinking about it* will make your life insane.

Debt-free living is the *best* kind of living. Of course, married life is great. And we love good food. And Jesus. Gosh, so much life to love!

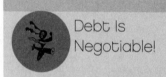

Debt Is Negotiable!

Yes, that's right! We know this from experience. If your credit card payments are past due or creditors are bugging the heck out of you, you might be able to strike a deal! When payments are WAY past due, usually creditors will cut a huge percentage off of what is owed just to rectify the problem. This might be another reason to hire the services of a financial counselor or law office; they can do the negotiations for you!

At least we think so.

Tootles!

Oh, and BTW: Pick up the Sex, Christianity, *and* Politics *books! We're fabulous there, too!*

>> The editors

PS: Let us know your thoughts. Write us at WeLoveWriting ForMatthew@yahoo.com.

Jesus Speaks of a Different Kind of Debt
[well, sort of!]

Then Peter came to him and asked, "Lord, how often should I forgive someone who sins against me? Seven times?"

"No!" Jesus replied, "seventy times seven!

"For this reason, the Kingdom of Heaven can be compared to a king who decided to bring his accounts up to date with servants who had borrowed money from him. In the process, one of his debtors was brought in who owed him millions of dollars. He couldn't pay, so the king ordered that he, his wife, his children, and everything he had be sold to pay the debt. But the man fell down before the king and begged him, 'Oh, sir, be patient with me, and I will pay it all.' Then the king was filled with pity for him, and he released him and forgave his debt.

"But when the man left the king, he went to a fellow servant who owed him a few thousand dollars. He grabbed him by the throat and demanded instant payment. His fellow servant fell down before him and begged for a little more time. 'Be patient and I will pay it,' he pleaded. But his creditor wouldn't wait. He had the man arrested and jailed until the debt could be paid in full.

"When some of the other servants saw this, they were very upset. They went to the king and told him what had happened. Then the king called in the man he had forgiven and said, 'You evil servant! I forgave you that tremendous debt because you pleaded with me. Shouldn't you have mercy on your fellow servant, just as I had mercy on you?' Then the angry king sent the man to prison until he had paid every penny.

"That's what my heavenly Father will do to you if you refuse to forgive your brothers and sisters in your heart." (Matthew 18:21-35)

A Poem About Money

We've come a long way in how we talk about money. And people across the world are *so* creative. So I thought it would be cool to remind you of a few terms we use [or used] instead of the word *money*.

Maybe you say *grand*; maybe you say *dollar*.
If you lived in England, you might call it an *Oxford scholar*.
When the age was more Victorian, they called it a *marigold*,
But today that term is obsolete, used only in a poem.
A few classics terms are *C-note*, *moola*, and *bucks*.
In Canada they say *loonie*, but I think that term sucks.
"I'm bringing home the *bacon*," you heard your Grampa say,
But did you know that *kale*, *cabbage*, and *lettuce* were also popular in his day?
You've probably heard the expression, "I'm rolling in the *dough*";
That means you've hit the *jackpot*, just in case you didn't know.
If you're into hip-hop, perhaps you call it *bills*.
You might also call it *paper* when you're spittin' out your thrills.

Back in the 1600s someone thought it would be
grand
To refer to it as *rhino* when there was lots of it in
hand.
Have you ever heard of *rocks*? Fred Flintstone called
it *clams*.
Coconut and *fish* were used; so was *iron man*.
So no matter how you say it, *peso*, *bob*, or *honey*,
It's all about one thing! And that one thing is *money*.

Do You Care?

[a conclusion]

Do all the good you can,
By all the means you can,
In all the ways you can,
In all the places you can,
At all the times you can,
To all the people you can,
As long as ever you can.

— John Wesley

Finally you're reading the last section. Hopefully you're still with me and not ready to kill me. It's a little overwhelming thinking this much about money, huh? Well, it is for me anyway.

Like I wrote in the introduction, I never thought I'd be writing a book on money. Though it's an interesting and extremely important topic, money just isn't a subject I have spent a great deal of time delving into before now [*of course, as you have read, my avoidance of all things money has caused me some problems in the area of, umm, my financial well-being*].

One reason for my poor financial situation is that I resisted honest conversations about my money habits—good and bad. When you're not talking honestly about your financial practices, you have a greater potential for utter financial disaster. Talking openly about money offers a person the opportunity for financial accountability, which is one of the best first steps in financial freedom.

I know, I know, I, too, have always been taught that money is a private issue. And to some extent, that's true; it is *private*. But just like the topics of Christianity, sex, and politics [yep, the other topics in the *What You Didn't Learn from Your Parents* series]—I'm not sure what I was thinking tackling all these topics at once—it's good for Christians to be talking about money. We need to be talking about our frustrations, weaknesses, successes, and abundances, especially as they relate to financial stewardship.

So in light of money conversations being good for us, let's have one!

Answer the following questions:

1. What do you believe is your biggest financial hang-up?

2. How healthy and godly do you perceive your current financial lifestyle?

3. How healthy and godly would your parents or friends perceive your financial lifestyle?

4. What financial area do you believe is your strongest? In your estimation, could you be saving more? If so, what's keeping you from doing so?

5. If you're one of the *millions* of twentysomethings who are in debt, what are you doing to get yourself out of debt?

6. What are you doing to plan for your retirement?

7. How do you define the word *generous?*

8. Would you consider yourself to be generous?

9. Now that you've almost finished this book, how has your perspective of stewardship changed?

10. How has the condition of your heart affected your handling [positively or negatively] of money?

The Heart and Money

In Philemon 1:6, Paul wrote, "You are generous because of your faith. And I am praying that you will really put your generosity to work, for in so doing you will come to an understanding of all the good things we can do for Christ."

Like most followers of Christ, I sometimes struggle with living generously. Despite having followed Jesus since I was under the age of five, when it comes to money, I still have this crazy tendency to think only of myself or how I am affected. Even in the simplest of financial choices, I stumble.

Last year I was at the gas station filling my car up with $2.89 per gallon midgrade fuel. As I watched the fuel gauge on the pump move past $35, I sighed. At the time, due to my weird income cycle, mainly because I am a writer, Jessica and I were experiencing a little financial drought. You know, *no money coming in*! Consequently, we were counting our pennies, wondering how we were going to pay all of our bills that month.

In the meantime, a lady pulled up to the pump next to mine. This woman, Betsy, was in her forties and had a couple of teeth missing, and her partially beat-up Pontiac Grand Prix was on its last wheels. As soon as she stepped out of her car, she came over to my side of the gas pump.

"Sir," she said in her deep Southern accent, "do you have a dollar I can use for gas? I have run out of money, and I'm trying to make it to Knoxville before dark."

"Umm, I don't have any cash," I replied, while thinking to myself that a dollar's worth of gas wouldn't get her to the other side of Nashville, let alone the 180 miles to Knoxville. I fumbled through my wallet, looking to see if indeed it was empty of cash.

"Would you use your card?" asked the lady rather brazenly.

I hesitated. My mind began racing. I thought about our dwindling bank account. I thought about how much that poor woman said she wanted to get to Knoxville. I thought about the bills Jessica and I needed to pay. I thought about how in need Betsy seemed. I wondered if Jessica would get upset with me, considering that we had just discussed our need to conserve the night before. I wondered if Betsy were an angel God was sending to test my willingness to serve him.

"I can use my check card," I said.

And to be perfectly honest, I said it in a rather begrudging tone.

"I'll put five dollars' worth of gas in your car."

"You wouldn't put ten, would you?" she asked.

"*Okay*, ten dollars."

"*Fifteen?*"

Though I don't believe I was *trying* to make a statement, the look on my face must have said what I was thinking loud and clear.

"No, I was just kidding; ten dollars is fine. Thank you."

"You're welcome!" I said as she began filling her car up with ten dollars' worth of gasoline. When she handed me the receipt, she thanked me again and we went our separate ways. On the way home, I began to feel like crap for hesitating. Okay, so I was a little mad that she was so persistent, too. But mostly I was angry that I hadn't given my money to her with a better attitude. *Why did I hesitate? Why didn't I offer to fill up*

Betsy's entire tank? I've been thinking about and researching God's thoughts about money for more than a month, and still I can't freely give of my money to a needy stranger. Why was it such a struggle for me to think beyond my own personal financial situation?

A couple of days later I was at the same gas station. As I walked into the convenience store to pay for my gas, Betsy pulled up to one of the other pumps. At first I was excited to see her. But my excitement turned to frustration as I watched Betsy use the same "I need to get to Knoxville" needy excuse on three or four of Exxon's patrons. All of them said no.

Either Betsy was a frequent *moneyless* traveler to Knoxville or she was a pretty convincing scam artist. I've decided—perhaps foolishly—to believe she's the former. But would it have made a difference? Is generosity about a real need being met or about the heart of the one being asked to fill the need?

Like most of the realities in the Christian life, our willingness to be generous with our money is often contingent on the condition of our hearts.

Okay, now let's finish that interview with David Briggs [yeah, the older guy who works at Willow Creek Community Church].

MPT: So like most things, our handling of money comes back to the condition of our hearts.

DAVID: No question about it. What I have found over the years is that we Christians get caught up in the act, whereas the Bible consistently talks about the attitude. In other words, it's about our hearts. Jesus wasn't interested in the doing; he was all about the why behind the doing. That was the only thing Christ ever zeroed in on — our motivation, our attitude, and our hearts.

MPT: When you consider the story of the woman in the Bible who put her last two coins in the offering plate, it seems Jesus wasn't interested in the amount given but in the willingness to give it all.

DAVID: Matthew, it amazes me how many times in the Scriptures giving is talked about without a need having been identified. [*Umm, this kind of relates to my story of Betsy, "the Knoxville Journeyer."*] I think the widow is a perfect example. Christ was sitting there watching. He called his disciples over and said, "Look at that widow." Of course, she ended up giving everything she had. The disciples looked at her two stinkin' mites and thought, *Why don't we tell her to keep her money, because she can use it more than the temple can? Two mites isn't really going to help much in the temple.* [*How many of you believe the disciples made a valid point?*] You see, Matthew, that's what happens when you start looking at giving from a needs base. We begin comparing. Most of us would stop short of giving because we don't see the need. But giving is a core part of our relationship with God.

MPT: David, when it comes to money, what are the key issues twenty and thirtysomethings are facing?

DAVID: I have spoken to twentysomethings on many occasions. In fact, I currently have a team of four twentysomethings working with me, trying to crack the "money" code with this demographic. The biggest problem I have seen is getting them to care. Now, I'm generalizing here; this certainly is not true 100 percent of the time. It's not hard to put together material that will help twentysomethings with their finances — that's not the big issue. The big issue is how to get them to care. If you can't get them to care, then everything you do downstream is of no effect at all. It's like having the perfect medicine and not being able to get someone to take it.

MPT: Why do you think we struggle to care?

DAVID: Unfortunately, this generation has only known abundance, Matthew. And even when they can't afford abundance, they have the mentality that "it's okay to borrow as much money as I want, whenever I want, so I can get whatever I want." They have never lived anything except "if I want it, I can have it — *now*." That's the way this generation is living, and they believe it is normal. In other words, what really matters to many of them is "what I can have right now." They've never been challenged; their parents have given them no reason to care. Before you can care, you need to have a reason to care. That, to me, is the single hardest nut to crack with this age group. Intellectually they may agree with you, but they won't care because they don't think they need to, and that's the way they have been raised. I am not saying that in a discouraging way; I am saying it in an observatory way.

MPT: Don't you think the availability of "stuff" is much greater now than it was ten to twenty years ago?

DAVID: It is the availability, but it is also the ability to get it [*he's talking about credit!*]. If you go back to our grandparents' generation, they had no concept of acquiring anything they did not have the money for. So if they ran out of money, they knew they could not have something. That is how they were raised. When many in today's generation don't have the money for something, they think, *What is the big deal with that? Today everybody buys stuff without money.* As soon as iPods came out, everybody got in line to buy one whether they had the money or not. That kind of thinking is destructive.

MPT: In some ways, they even sacrifice basic necessities to get the iPod.

DAVID: I don't think that's sacrificing, Matthew. There's no sacrifice when you go borrow the money so you can have an iPod. That's not sacrifice.

MPT: That's true; however, I know I have friends who will sacrifice paying their rent in order to buy something extravagant, or they will have an extreme amount of debt and add to it to buy something they don't really need.

DAVID: Sacrifice means you have to care, Matthew. If someone says, "I am short on my rent, but what is the big deal with that?" it is not a sacrifice unless it cost you something. I contend that it's not costing anybody anything right now. It will cost them something in the future, but they are okay about the future, thinking, *Why should I bother about the future? I'll just take care of it then.* I hope your readers won't take my words as condemning; I am just observing what I have seen in people I've talked to. And it's understandable that people in this generation think this way because it is what they've been fed.

MPT: David, we live in a time when much of our lives revolve around seeking out success. A high school education isn't good enough anymore; we have to go to college and get a degree — but without the guarantee of success. Now you almost have to have a master's degree to be successful in the world's eyes. So by the time we get to a place where we are ready to be successful, we are already $25,000 in debt [at least!] because of our schooling. How does *that* play into the whole concept of stewardship and caring?

DAVID: Two different questions. Most don't have any clue about what stewardship really means. I think if you stopped ten twentysomethings in downtown Chicago or Nashville and asked them, "What does stewardship mean to you?" the vast majority would say it's the word churches use when they are trying to raise money. Sadly, the whole idea of living as a steward is totally foreign because living as a steward really assumes that your number one priority is to live for the best interest of someone other than yourself. In this case, many twentysomethings don't have any *masters*; they bow down to no one except *themselves*. The whole idea of being under the authority of one greater than them is not only a foreign concept; it is somewhat repulsive to them. You can't grasp the concept of stewardship until you buy in to the fact that you have to answer to somebody — *the Master.*

MPT: Let's change topics here. Do you think young adults depend too much on their parents? I mean, kids are moving back in with their parents after college, or they are depending on them financially. I myself have asked my parents on a couple of occasions for financial help. Twenty or thirty years ago this concept would have been seen as crazy.

DAVID: It's funny you should mention that. Let me give you two statistics that I stumbled onto not too long ago. Ten years ago, bankruptcy filings among people ages eighteen to twenty-five were less than 1 percent, and now they are more than 5 percent. So eighteen- to twenty-five-year-olds are five times more likely to declare bankruptcy than they were ten years ago. Also, in the last five years, adult-age children that are either living with their parents or are financially dependent upon their parents has gone up 70 percent. Essentially, this is delayed normal adulthood. I believe the reason for this is twofold. One is the idea, like I discussed earlier, of having anything you want when you want it, rather than saving up for it or working for it. This has caused a mentality of living for today. When you live day to day, you do not build the kind of structure that prepares you for leaving the nest. The other problem is that this is the first generation growing up without a clue financially whose parents didn't have a clue financially. So they have no role models, and their parents are enabling them as much as they themselves want to be enabled. They are both equally dysfunctional and so they kind of depend on each other. It isn't just that the twentysomethings aren't leaving; it is that the parents never taught them how to leave.

MPT: I see your point. This is the first generation that was raised by people who lived with a substantial amount of debt, huh?

DAVID: And those parents didn't have a clue what was going on financially, and that further handicaps the twentysomethings. They aren't aware of what they don't know, and they get so far down into the hole that out of desperation, when they are in their thirties, they just explode. And someone, maybe a church or a parent, has to pick up the pieces after ten years of a financial downward spiral.

MPT: When you talk with people about tithing and giving to the church or a ministry, how do you go about teaching this?

DAVID: When I talk about the spiritual aspect of money, I talk about the three Gs. One G is giving; however, we get so caught up in the church today in the act of giving — as we talked about before — that I think we miss the mark on what Jesus was teaching. Despite the popularity of this belief, Jesus didn't really come to teach giving; he came to teach the other two Gs that we should be focusing on. One is generosity and the other is gratefulness. He didn't come to teach us to do a better job of giving our money. He came to teach us what to be like. He wants us to be generous people and to be grateful people.

An analogy I often use to explain this is a story about my son. He's twenty-three and loves to fish. But I hate to fish. However, I like to spend time with him, so sometimes we go fishing. We are standing beside the river doing something identical — you know, we're both holding poles and casting our lines into the same stream. The difference, though, is that he loves it and I hate it. So he's the fisherman, and I am simply fishing. Therefore, my son is more likely not only to enjoy the experience but also to catch more fish. You see, Matthew, Jesus came not to teach us how to give but to teach us how to be generous and grateful. When we are generous and grateful, then out of that generosity and gratefulness follow a number of things, including actions expressing generosity and gratefulness. And then we will be givers involved with

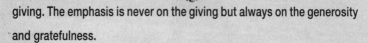

giving. The emphasis is never on the giving but always on the generosity and gratefulness.

Matthew, if we make *giving* our emphasis, we begin asking silly questions, such as, "If I give 9.8 percent, is that good enough? Will God be satisfied with me?" That's nonsense. Once we embrace generosity, we throw percentages out the window. I think so often Jesus looks at us and says, "You're missing the entire point, people. I don't care about that stuff. I want to know whether or not you're generous people. Because if you become generous, then I won't ever have to have a conversation with you about giving. You're just going to do it because of who you are and because it's in the nature of your heart to do so."

MPT: Thanks, David, for talking through this with me.
DAVID: No problem.

For God is not unfair. He will not forget how hard you have worked for him and how you have shown your love to him by caring for other Christians, as you still do. (Hebrews 6:10)

When God's children are in need, be the one to help them out. And get into the habit of inviting guests home for dinner or, if they need lodging, for the night. (Romans 12:13)

Don't forget to do good and to share what you have with those in need, for such sacrifices are very pleasing to God. (Hebrews 13:16)

But if anyone has enough money to live well and sees a brother or sister in need and refuses to help — how can God's love be in that person?

Dear children, let us stop just saying we love each other; let us really show it by our actions. It is by our actions that we know we are living in the truth, so we will be confident when we stand before the Lord. (1 John 3:17-19)

"If you give, you will receive. Your gift will return to you in full measure, pressed down, shaken together to make room for more, and running over. Whatever measure you use in giving — large or small — it will be used to measure what is given back to you." (Luke 6:38)

Remember this — a farmer who plants only a few seeds will get a small crop. But the one who plants generously will get a generous crop. You must each make up your own mind as to how much you should give. Don't give reluctantly or in response to pressure. For God loves the person who gives cheerfully. And God will generously provide all you need. Then you will always have everything you need and plenty left over to share with others. As the Scriptures say,

> "Godly people give generously to the poor.
>   Their good deeds will never be forgotten." (2 Corinthians 9:6-9)

And I have been a constant example of how you can help the poor by working hard. You should remember the words of the Lord Jesus: "It is more blessed to give than to receive." (Acts 20:35)

Since you excel in so many ways — you have so much faith, such gifted speakers, such knowledge, such enthusiasm, and such love for us — now I want you to excel also in this gracious ministry of giving. I am not saying you must do it, even though the other churches are eager to do it. This is one way to prove your love is real.

You know how full of love and kindness our Lord Jesus Christ was. Though he was very rich, yet for your sakes he became poor, so that by his poverty he could make you rich. (2 Corinthians 8:7-9)

Ideas For Your Generosity!

Who to give to?	Who are they?	Where can I get more info?
World Vision	Child-sponsor agency that will help you adopt a needy child in a Third World country.	www.worldvision.org
Mercy Ministries	They assist women with life-controlling problems like drugs, alcohol, cutting, eating disorders, unplanned pregnancies, and depression.	www.Mercyministries.org
St. Jude Children's Research Hospital	The leading research hospital treating children with cancer.	www.stjude.org
Shriners of North America	They provide children under the age of eighteen with free ortho-pedic and burn care in all of the twenty-two Shriners hospitals.	www.shrinershq.org
The Salvation Army	They provide disaster relief, AIDS assistance, refugee relief, and many other volunteer programs.	www.salvationarmyusa.org
American Red Cross	They provide many different programs, from blood donation to disaster relief. They are usually the first relief organization on the scene after a major disaster.	www.redcross.org
One	This is a campaign to eliminate extreme poverty and AIDS across the world.	www.one.org
Make-A-Wish	They grant wishes to children with life threatening conditions to promote hope and joy.	www.wish.org
Young Life	They meet kids where they are and provide a Christlike example to influence this receptive portion of society.	www.younglife.org
Habitat for Humanity	This organization builds afford-able homes for needy families who would otherwise not be able to own a home.	www.habitat.org
Your local church	Umm, supporting Christian minis-tries through the local church is important!	Varies
Your friends in need	This is pretty self-explanatory. If you have friends who are in need, help them out!	Varies — probably start with www.myspace.com

In Conclusion, How to Care?

Do you care? No, really, do you care?

I know I sound a little like a Hallmark card. However, as silly as I know this question might seem to some of you, it's one I feel is rather fitting for the ending of this book.

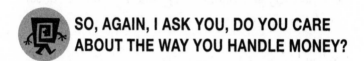 **SO, AGAIN, I ASK YOU, DO YOU CARE ABOUT THE WAY YOU HANDLE MONEY?**

There isn't a list of yes-or-no questions you can answer in order to know whether or not you care. However, you can be sure that whether or not you care will be evident in these three areas:

- Your spending of money
- Your saving of money
- Your generosity with money

All of these areas are important to God. So when it comes to thinking about these three areas, honesty is of utmost importance. *Duh!* As I've stated before in this book [and it's also something David Briggs mentioned in my interview with him], the handling of our finances flows from the condition of our hearts. That's why your care or lack of care would be evident in these three areas.

You see, your actions within these three areas usually reveal what's important to you, the kinds of things you value, your understanding of stewardship, your attitude toward money, and, most important, the "financial" condition of your heart [or, in other words, *how your heart thinks about money*]. Our actions [in every area of our lives] are a thermometer of sorts for our hearts.

But there's a catch to all of this....

No matter who you are, if you're honest about your financial lifestyle, you'd have to admit that you could indeed care more. Don't be shy about your complete and utter ability to be lame with money; all of us could improve. I certainly know I could. Some of us are more *careless* than others, but for the most part, each of our hearts, as they relate to all things money, can certainly find areas to improve upon. More than likely you could admit a little shortage of caring yourself.

Yep, that would mean you don't care enough. Don't be embarrassed by your lack of financial concern. Caring isn't brain surgery. It's not like it's something you can't begin to embrace; in fact, you could begin right now.

Yes, you could. Now, you might be thinking, *How does one who suffers from a lack of care begin to care? And so quickly?* Well, you can be sure of one thing: There isn't a magic potion you can drink that will make you suddenly care.

And there's nothing I can do to make you care.

You just do.

Or you don't.

Period.

However, I can offer this. About two years ago, my wife and I began to care. Sure, I had attempted to care before. In fact, I even believed I did care a few times. But my actions revealed otherwise. One night, a few short months before my wife and I got married, I became overwhelmed by my financial situation.

Usually when this would happen, I'd suffer in silence. Yeah, I'd pray, but then I'd just take the anxiety I was feeling about my financial situation and attempt to turn it into perseverance and wisdom. This is difficult to do. The last thing I want to do is sugarcoat this stuff or make it sound like I'm preaching at you. I mean, some days I tell myself this stuff and I hardly believe it. Many times I would become so exasperated by how

I was handling my finances that I would try to make changes to my habits. That didn't always work, but I truly believe I tried to care. But honestly, I didn't know how to care. My anxiety was almost always more about my bad situation than it was about what God thought about money. I was clueless.

But something was different about that day, six months before getting married. I was overwhelmed by my financial situation; that much was the same. But I resisted the urge to suffer in silence. Instead, I called Jessica. Though she knew long before that day that I was in debt, that was pretty much all she knew. So over the phone, we began having a very difficult conversation about money.

I'd be lying if I said it was a simple talk, one without its share of frustrating moments. To say the least, that talk was excruciating. Jessica cried. I cried. She voiced her concern. I explained my situation. I told her everything. And then we prayed. The dirty details of that conversation are a private matter between my wife and me, but I want you to know this:

>> **For the first time in my life,** I felt God beginning to open my eyes to how much he cared about money and how I was mishandling his money. For years, I believed God just wanted his 10 percent, and the rest was mine to use however I wanted. So the first step I had to take toward caring was making a confession, telling God I was sorry for taking the **possessions he gave me for granted.** <<

Then I asked for help. After that, I needed to allow what I had learned about God's perspective on money to make an impact on my habits. Trust me; that was a process because I LOVED being able to do what I wanted with "my" money.

Do Jessica and I still struggle? Yes. In fact, hardly a month goes by that we don't have to confess again and ask God [and one another] for help, guidance, *and a whole lot of patience* on the journey.

But we care. Of course, you and I both know we're not perfect at caring. And we're not totally out of debt yet. But we care. We're in the process of learning that we don't want our financial situation to control us. We're also learning that we don't want to control our financial situation. We're striving toward simply being good stewards of what God allows to come into our lives, asking him to teach us how to use it to help his kingdom.

I know some of this conclusion sounds like Christian jargon. But the snag is, unlike other areas of life where God leaves room for gray throughout Scripture, with money he's a lot clearer. He gives us a guideline to strive toward. Is it etched in stone without flexibility? Of course not; God isn't a stickler.

So I'll ask one more time. Do you care? [I'll sing it: Do you CAAAARRRRRE?!?!?] The frustrating thing is this: All of the information in this book is pointless if you don't. I know I could have put that at the beginning. But then you wouldn't have read it. I'm not a money expert, but I'm certainly not stupid! Anyway, the bottom line is that the process of living a good, healthy financial life starts with choosing to care.

We're called to care.

GOD CERTAINLY DOES.

Notes

Introduction

1. Juliet Hindell, "Japan's War on Germs and Smells," *BBC News,* May 30, 1999, http://news.bbc.co.uk/1/hi/programmes/from_our_own_correspondent/354321.stm.
2. Federal Reserve Bank of Atlanta, "Spotting Counterfeit Currency," http://www.frbatlanta.org/invoke_brochure.cfm?objectid=83FD4205-9AF0-11D5-898400508BB89A83&method=display_body.
3. Federal Reserve Bank of Atlanta.

Section One: Rethinking Money

1. Pew Research Center, "Are We Happy Yet?" February 13, 2006, http://pewresearch.org/social/pack.php?PackID=1.
2. Dictionary.com, s.v. "Steward."

Section Two: Money Basics You Need to Know!

1. Liz Pulliam Weston, "Your 20s: See How Your Wealth Measures Up," http://articles.moneycentral.msn.com/CollegeAndFamily/MoneyInYour20s/Your20sSeeHowYourWealthMeasuresUp.aspx.
2. Weston.
3. Rashmikant Patel, "Smart Banking," AskMen.com, http://www.askmen.com/money/investing_60/63b_investing.html.
4. "Smart Banking," http://www.taxmatters.afsb1.com/cgi-bin/taxmatters/ADDITIONAL.INFO.PAGE.DISPLAY?page_id=SmartBanking.
5. "Retirement and Estate Planning," InvestorGuide.com, http://www.investorguide.com/links-dir-retirement.html.
6. "Personal Finance Terms You Should Know," *Kiplingler's Personal Finance,* http://www.kiplinger.com/personalfinance/basics/glossary/.
7. United States Department of the Treasury, "FAQs: Currency," http://www.treasury.gov/education/faq/currency/production.shtml; Fact Monster, "Facts About U.S. Money," 2005, http://www.factmonster.com/ipka/A0774850.html.

Section Three: Spending and Saving

1. Eric Tyson, *Personal Finance for Dummies,* 2nd ed. (New York: IDG Books Worldwide, 1997), 55.
2. Michael Bluejay, "Saving Electricity," http://michaelbluejay.com/electricity/.
3. Insure.com, "5 Ways to Get Auto Insurance Discounts," http://articles.moneycentral.msn.com/Insurance/InsureYourCar/5waysToGetAutoInsuranceDiscounts.aspx.
4. Larry Magid, "Strikebound Lean on Technology," CBS News, December 22, 2005, http://www.cbsnews.com/stories/2005/12/22/scitech/pcanswer/main1156676.shtml.

Section Four: The Stuff Grown-Ups Do

1. Mary Randolph, JD, "Make a Will," *Wills & Estate Planning*, http://www.nolo.com/article.cfm/pg/1/objectId/C7217F40-D912 -490A-920D6C7C3B29FDDC/catId/FD1795A9-8049-422C -9087838F86A2BC2B/309/CHK/.
2. Kendra Inman, "Channel 4's Stress Survival Guide to . . . Housebuying," *4Health*, http://www.channel4.com/health/microsites/0-9/4health/stress/cws _housebuying.html.
3. "Mortgage for Beginners," http://www.forbeginners.info/mortgage/mortgage -basics.htm.
4. The American Institute of Certified Public Accountants, "AICPA Media Center: Startling Facts on Financial Literacy," http://www.aicpa.org/ MediaCenter/Startling_Facts.htm.
5. The American Institute of Certified Public Accountants.

Section Five: The Credit Card

1. DMB Financial, "Did You Know?" 2006, http://dmbfinance.com/.

About the Author

MATTHEW PAUL TURNER is the best-selling author of *The Christian Culture Survival Guide* and *Provocative Faith*. Before he began speaking and writing full-time, he served as editor of CCM and music and entertainment editor for Crosswalk.com. He and his wife, Jessica, live in Nashville, Tennessee. To find out more about Matthew, visit his website at www.MatthewPaulTurner.com.